Line
Quality Assurance
Nursing Service

Quality of Care Assessment and Assurance

Quality of Care Assessment and Assurance

AN ANNOTATED BIBLIOGRAPHY WITH A POINT OF VIEW

Norbert Hirschhorn, M.D.
Joel H. Lamstein, S.M.
Jeanne McCormack, Ed.M.
Susan F. Klein, M.P.H.

John Snow Public Health Group, Inc.
141 Tremont Street
Boston, Ma. 02111

G. K. Hall & Co.   Boston

This publication was supported by contract #290-76-0012 of the Department of Health, Education and Welfare. Its contents do not necessarily reflect the views of the DHEW.

G. K. Hall & Co.
Medical Publications Division
70 Lincoln St.
Boston, Ma. 02111

78 79 80 81/ 8 7 6 5 4 3 2 1

Hirschhorn, Norbert.
    Quality of care assessment and assurance.

    (Contemporary issues in health sciences)
    At head of title: John Snow Public Health Group, Inc.
    1. Medical care—Evaluation—Bibliography. 2. Medical care—Quality control—Bibliography. Lamstein, Joel H., joint author, I. McCormack, Jeanne, joint author. II. Klein, Susan F., joint author. III. John Snow Public Health Group, Inc. IV. Title. V. Series.
Z6673.4.H57   [RA394]   362.1   78-14285
ISBN 0-8161-2123-0

Contents

Introduction

This is a bibliography with a bias. Hundreds of articles, monographs and books have been written about Quality of Care Assessment and Assurance (Q/Caa) in ambulatory medicine. Nevertheless, it is still difficult to know just what good care comprises (*Quality*), how to measure it accurately (*Assessment*), or how to make sure it stays good (*Assurance*). It is especially true of ambulatory care that only tenuous links are found between what is done for a patient, and what finally happens to that person. Yet most Q/Caa schemes continue to examine the specific, technical interactions between a provider and the patient; but they fail to measure, much less assure, quality. Two factors contribute to this failure: 1) medical care is delivered increasingly by organizations with multiple layers of staff and systems; and 2) the scope and complexity of medical services and technology have increased almost beyond control. Whether all this complexity is beneficial is doubtful; that its cost is high is not. Despite medical advances, millions of persons in this country are still unable to get simple, compassionate care, or achieve prevention of serious physical and mental afflictions.

The articles chosen for annotation in this bibliography support the following points of view:

1. Q/Caa must be an organization-wide affair and not simply a review of medical charts.

2. A better Q/Caa system is not enough. It must be tied to an explicit definition of what a particular health care organization is trying to accomplish which, in turn, must be appropriate to the needs of the people served by the organization.

3. While the attributes of appropriate care are still debated, some types of care have been proved to make a difference in the outcome of illness and in the maintenance of health. They are:

    a) removal of subtle as well as obvious barriers to care;
    b) availability and continuity of needed services;
    c) delivery of care in a compassionate and dignified manner;
    d) a minimum of major errors in diagnosis and use of drugs;

e) a strong emphasis on use of proven methods of prevention and screening; and

f) the maintenance of cost-effective and managerially efficient operations.

Other attributes of quality may emerge later to meet the requirements of the time and new knowledge.

4.   Each of the attributes mentioned can be expanded into a series of criteria which may be quantified—so much waiting time, so many percent immunized, etc.—and therefore assessed. Operational steps can be taken to assure that targets are either met or revised.

5.   It is clear that Q/Caa, to be at all useful in improving health and delivery of health care, must be an integral part of planning and managing health care systems.

This bibliography is organized into four categories and several subcategories. The sequence of the annotations within the categories is a deliberate one; it is intended to lead the reader to the conclusions listed above. We have also not shied from interpreting many of the articles. Our own views are signaled by the word "Comment."

Philosophy and Review

Definitions of Quality

Hiatt, H. H. "Protecting the Medical Commons: Who is Responsible?" *The New England Journal of Medicine* 293(1975): 235−241.

This article discusses the finite resources available for health and summarizes the choices of medical technology and medical processes which must be made.

1.   Trained prehospital rescue units resuscitated 301 patients with heart attacks. Forty-two left the hospital (5 brain damaged) and survived for a mean of thirteen months. Was it worth it? How do we tell?

2.   Nearly a dozen major surgical procedures have been abandoned in recent years because they proved worthless. Ninety percent of the one million yearly tonsillectomies are probably unnecessary. Oral hypoglycemic agents are given to 1.4 million Americans but are probably more harmful than helpful. The treatment of acute pulmonary edema was as successful on a general medical ward as in intensive care and at much lower cost. Coronary angiography leading to coronary artery surgery for every American with heart disease could cost up to 100 billion dollars a year. Even if proved useful, the decision to use such technology must still be made.

3.   Carelessness in promulgating simple immunizations and prevention programs is causing an increase or no change in the incidence of polio, measles, dental decay, black lung disease, infant mortality in the poor, and environmentally caused cancer.

4.   Poor, underserved children have considerable prevalence of anemia (ages ½ to 3 years, over 25%), poor vision (25%), and middle ear disease (20%) with hearing loss (7%) and poor performance in school.

The individual physician cannot possibly take all factors into account when treating patients. But the standards of therapy must eventually be based on the rational use of all resources, dictated by continuing research, cost effectiveness, and technical and ethical issues.

Cullen, D. J.; Ferrara, L. C.; and Briggs, B. A. et al. "Survival, Hospitalization Charges and Follow-Up Results in Critically Ill Patients." *The New England Journal of Medicine* 294(1976): 982–987.

These statistics are derived from a one year study of 226 critically ill patients who were admitted consecutively:

226		
164 Dead	11 Still hospitalized	51 Home 27 Recovered

Eighty-three percent of blood transfusion costs were spent on the deceased, 17% on the survivors. The use of limited resources for the management of critically ill patients will be controlled either directly or indirectly through medical-governmental policy decisions since the level of intensive care, if applied to all critically ill patients in the U.S., would cost 46 billion dollars per year.

Sidel, V. W. "Quality for Whom? Effects of Professional Responsibility for Quality of Health Care on Equity." *Bulletin of the New York Academy of Medicine* 52(1976): 164–176.

1.   "Quality" is in the eye of the beholder, and a professional's view is often inconsistent with the consumer's and is not necessarily correct.
2.   A definition of "quality" reflects a statement of goals which in health care often reflects the predominant view of the provider.

3. Current measurements of "quality" are difficult in terms of precision, reliability, and replicability. Sometimes only easily measured indicators are measured, whether relevant or not.
4. The process to outcome link is often nonexistent.
5. Audits can detract time from service delivery; an emphasis on technical aspects subtly decreases accessibility.
6. Measurement of short-term outcomes can lead to a short sighted view of health care.
7. A definition of "quality" should take into account the barriers that keep consumers from playing a role in health care systems:
    a) the heterogeneity of the urban community;
    b) ignorance of personal fitness;
    c) feelings of powerlessness; and
    d) feelings of intimidation by professionals.

Navarro, V. "The Underdevelopment of Health of Working America: Causes, Consequences and Possible Solutions." *American Journal of Public Health* 66(1976): 538–547.

A Marxist view of ill health: social class correlates with morbidity and mortality in the U.S.; the working class is in a much worse situation. These findings are attributed not to perverse lifestyles but to occupational hazards, alienation, boredom, and powerlessness. Dwelling on life-styles is a rationale used by those in power (upper-classes) to divert attention from the social/political causes of illness.

Conover, P. W. "Social Class and Chronic Illness." *International Journal of Health Services* 3(1973): 357–368.

The relationship between social class and illness has been subject to several different and opposing interpretations. Taking

data from the 1965–1967 National Health Survey, the author eluci-
dates several aspects of this relationship:

1. There is a strong association between income and measures
    of chronic disease. The poorest group demonstrates a 50 to
    100% greater incidence of chronic illness and resulting dis-
    ability.
2. Age is an overriding cause and correlate of chronic illness.
3. Approximately half the population of the United States and
    85% of people over 65 have some chronic illness.
4. Limitation of activity resulting from chronic illness is minor
    in most instances.
5. Differences in incidence of chronic illness are strongly re-
    lated to income, but not racial groupings.
6. These differences are not, as some observers have claimed,
    due to a tendency of lower classes to "overreact" to chronic
    illness, but simply to poverty, lack of access to health ser-
    vices, and to fewer amenities (health insurance, sick leave)
    to ameliorate ill health.
7. These relationships are true for twelve selected chronic con-
    ditions, none of which are commonly thought of as class-
    related. These findings clearly have implications for national
    health policy.

Carter, J. E. Speech on Preventive Health Care. Presented to American Public Health Assoc., 19 October 1976, at Miami Beach,
Florida.

President Carter's health care goals for the United States are:

1. preventive programs, especially oriented to neighborhoods
    and communities;
2. national health insurance stressing both catastrophic and
    prenatal/infant care benefits;
3. health and nutrition education in public schools;
4. attack on environmental carcinogens;
5. more biomedical research;
6. bureaucratic streamlining;

7.   alternative delivery systems (HMOs, rural group practices);
8.   cleanup of Medicaid mills; and
9.   scholarships to women, minorities, and poor people so that they will pursue careers in medicine and thereby promote inner city and rural practice.

"National Health Planning and Resources Development Act of 1974." Public Law 93–641, 93rd Congress, S.2994, January 4, 1975.

Public Law 93–641 passed by Congress in 1974 is known as the "National Health Planning and Resources Development Act of 1974." National Health priorities (Section 1502) promulgated by this law (to be translated into quantifiable targets) are linked to the three overall purposes of Public Law 93–641 which are equal access, improved quality of health care, and cost constraint. The priorities and linkages are:

The Section 1502 Priorities	Equal Access	Quality of Care	Cost Constraint
1. Primary care for the underserved	X		
2. Coordination of health services		X	X
3. Medical group practices		X	X
4. Physician assistants	X		X
5. Sharing of support services			X
6. Improving quality		X	
7. Appropriate levels of care	X	X	X
8. Disease prevention	X	X	X
9. Uniform reporting systems			X
10. Health education	X	X	X

Comment: Since the priorities are to be specified by operational terms and numerical targets, they will increasingly form the basis of Quality of Care Assessments.

Chamberlin, R. W., and Radebaugh, J. F. "Delivery of Primary Health Care—Union Style. A Critical Review of the Robert F. Kennedy Plan for the United Farm Workers of America." *The New England Journal of Medicine* 294(1976): 641–645.

This is a sharply focused article on the attributes of quality of care as defined by a militant rural labor union.

First, the road to health is defined in societal terms:

"People are healthy not because of good hospitals or good doctors or good medicine . . . A healthy body demands that you have decent living conditions and decent working conditions. '(Ill health is) a symptom of poverty and powerlessness.'"

Second, the activities of health clinics stress self-sufficiency, primary preventive care, health education, outreach and active involvement in environmental improvement and union activism. Medical technology is kept to a minimum and folk medicine is interwoven. Third, a strong emphasis is placed on the family health worker, an outreach social activist and ombudsman. Fourth, physicians and nurses are entirely subordinate to the union lay committees, earn little money, work long hours, and do many housekeeping chores. Fifth, the clinics operate to eliminate cultural, economic, and physical barriers to access.

The clinics are greatly successful in acquiring the support and approval of their clients. However, they are not adequately responsive to the needs of professionals. Professionals do not have power, a voice in decisions, and an option to continue their education. They suffer from low pay, long hours, and "incompetent practices due to understaffing."

Comment:
1. The health philosophy and goals stated in this article are reminiscent of those of the Settlement Houses in our big cities

in the early twentieth century. This period was before medical technology became dominant.

2.   "Quality" takes on a markedly different face when defined and controlled by consumers with a political focus.

3.   Is provider control necessary to keep a health system working? Or must the government intervene?

The Role of Quality of Care Assessment and Assurance

Brook, R. H., and Avery, A. D. *Quality Assessment: Issues of Definition and Measurement.* Santa Monica, Calif.: The Rand Corporation, 1976.

Brook and Avery have thought and written extensively on the issue of quality assessment. This Rand monograph summarizes their current views:

1. The definition of "Quality of care" must include the adequacy of:
    a) technical management (diagnosis, treatment);
    b) the "art of care" (or caring-compassion-communication);
    c) efficiency of care (costs, convenience);
    d) accessibility of care; and
    e) availability of care.
    Most assessments only cover technical management, doctor patient interactions, and single visits; all encounters with the patient over the entire episode of illness should be included.

2. Quality of care assessment should be focused on three types of visits: preventive-maintenance, acute, and chronic. Even an entity such as hypertension should be audited across this spectrum.

3. A broad organizational view of multiple variables is needed; such a model is 5 to 10 years away. Brook and Avery distinguish this view as a *quality assurance program* as distinct from current audits which are *quality assessment studies*.

4. In ambulatory care it is more reliable to conduct assessment studies from a defined sign, symptom, or problem (fever, chest pain, etc.) rather than by diagnoses, given the level of diagnosis and recording.

5. If diagnoses or problems are used as the sample frame, those likely to be a problem area should be tackled as a priority —for example, excessive use of injectables.

6. Since the level of care—even by the same provider—tends to vary by condition, it is possible to pick "good perfor-

mance" conditions and put on a public face of good quality
medicine.

Brook, R. H.; Williams, K. N.; and Avery, A. D. "Quality Assurance
Today and Tomorrow: Forecast for the Future." *Annals of Internal
Medicine* 85(1976): 809–817.

This article attempts to predict what shape Quality Assessment and Assurance will or should take over the next decade. A
number of recommendations are made:
1. The "art-of-care" (as opposed to the technical skills) should
    be studied and its effect on health compared to technical
    aspects.
2. No "ideal" quality system is likely and only efforts that are
    proved to improve care should be undertaken.
3. Improvement in physician education (licensure, mandatory
    continuing education) is unlikely to improve care since most
    poor care comes from not doing well known, easy medical
    interventions such as immunization, diagnosis and treatment
    of hypertension and anemia. Education should not be stressed
    as the method of assurance.
4. Major research is needed in five areas:
    a) development of "decision-tree" (branched logic) process
       criteria;
    b) diagnostic taxonomies developed by risk groups such as
       age, race, and prior illness;
    c) measurement of short-term or proximate outcomes;
    d) measurement of care as perceived by clients; and
    e) research into public attitudes to health and health promo-
       tion.
5. A nation-wide quality assurance system should be estab-
    lished with extensive data linkages and sharing, and should
    be tied to financial incentives or disincentives.
6. Valid outcome measures must include functional capacity,
    and comfort and satisfaction of the client.
7. Recording and data sources constrain assessment. The au-
    thors do not believe recordkeeping must be improved just for

assessment, but also for logical care. It may even be cheaper to go back and get data from patients.

8.   Criteria for assessment should follow sparse logic and good decision making rather than all-inclusive "laundry listing." Many criteria are due for revision; some are based on mistaken assumptions of willingness to pay for care.

9.   The "priority [in quality assessment] lies on the side of correcting the major deficiencies in quality of medical care, wherever they may lie."

Brook, R. H.; Williams, K. N.; and Avery, A. D. "Quality Assurance in the 20th Century: Will It Lead to Improved Health in the 21st?" Santa Monica, Calif.: The Rand Corporation, 1975.

1.   Quality Assurance, by 1980, will cost 2 to 5% of each health care dollar or 2 to 5 *billion* dollars.

2.   Most assurance programs have measured technical care (as recorded in the medical record) and not real caring. Research priorities must be in the art of caring.

3.   Quality of care—whenever measured—is not up to stated standards, and the deficit is caused by physicians' behavior and characteristics of the medical care system, not to the current level of physician knowledge or training.

4.   If quality of care actually came up to current "acceptable" criteria, hospital costs would increase 50% (10 billion dollars per year) and ambulatory costs 250% (40 billion dollars per year). If even better recording is mandated, office visits would increase in time by 33%.

5.   Current methods of audit are either notoriously imprecise or too inclusive.

6.   Audits that examine only one element of care, such as care of hypertension, can disrupt the whole system by improper emphasis on that particular condition.

7.   Proximate-outcome, decision-analysis, staging, and other new methods to assess outcomes are needed; but in light of current knowledge, simple audits of process criteria must suffice for the next 5 years.

8.   Diagnostic procedures are at least two-edged: they pick up more false positives as their sensitivity is increased, and there is a high cost to detect one true positive.
9.   Self-care must be taught increasingly.

Roemer, M. I. "Hospital Utilization and the Health Care System." *American Journal of Public Health* 66(1976): 953–955.

This editorial is a potent argument for utilization review and cost containment as a rationale for quality assessment. The evidence is that medical procedures, surgery, and therefore costs will increase as the number of physicians increases. In a study of two health insurance plans, only 15% of utilization rates was dependent on consumer demand and other consumer variables. The balance (85%) was attributable to features of the health care system, including physicians' practice habits.

Densen, P. M. "Public Accountability and Reporting Systems in Medicare and Other Health Programs." *The New England Journal of Medicine* 298(1973): 401–406.

The author provides a societal basis for quality of care assessment. The "public" has the right to know how monies for medical care are spent: the distribution of the services bought, the performance of the providers, and the general quality of the care.

For this information to be collected and disseminated, decisions must be made on the criteria for assessment, on the means of gathering data, and on data control. Such information is both a precursor and a prerequisite for national health insurance.

Comment: It is obvious that government will represent the "public."

Ginzberg, E. "Notes on Evaluating the Quality of Medical Care." *The New England Journal of Medicine* 292(1975): 366–368.

1. Quality assurance should be limited to controlled settings at first, such as in hospitals, and all methodological problems should be worked out there.
2. Rather than develop broad standards of "quality," we should identify a few major types of bad practice and work on developing a remedial program.
3. Data and record systems that support "quality" and quality assurance should be developed before launching into audits.

McNerney, W. J. "The Quandary of Quality Assessment." *The New England Journal of Medicine* 295(1976): 1505–1511.

Although the author confusedly interchanges "assessment" and "assurance," he basically asks "Why do assessment?" His argument is familiar: medical (illness) care alone has only a small effect on morbidity and mortality. One model cited identifies five variables which affect health: genetics, environment, society, lifestyle, and medical care. The last may influence health with a weight of 6%, but it is most costly. Therefore, the areas of efficiency, utilization, payment methods, planning, management, access, and quality of life-styles should be emphasized in assessment programs.

Greene, R. *Assuring Quality in Medical Care: The State of the Art.* Cambridge, Ma.: Ballinger Publishing Co., 1976.

This book has the keenest and most precise analysis of the current state of the art.

Chapter 2: The various methods of quality of care assessment all share in one or more of the following disadvantages:

1. an inability to measure important variables such as provider warmth, or a tendency to confuse divergent variables, such as client vs. provider-reported outcomes;
2. poor replicability;
3. poor sampling and data base;
4. poor reproducibility of judgments;
5. high costs;
6. technical difficulties;
7. few links between medical process and outcomes; and
8. general failure to improve provider performance.

Chapter 3: Assessments are directed to varying purposes: utilization review, education, provider profiles, "goal survey," fraud detection, efficiency, client satisfaction, provider-client interactions ("caring function"), and research. Assessment of primary care differs considerably from measuring hospital-based care in that variables are less well-delineated, more susceptible to unknown influences, less well-categorized, and yield "softer" data. Most primary care in the U.S. is delivered by solo practitioners. Will *they* be audited?

Chapter 4: The present range of provider performance in the U.S. often falls short of standards selected by those investigating the subject. Much of the poor performance, however, is due to failure to apply traditional skills learned in medical school, or to "systems failures" (coordination of care, communication, management).

Chapter 7: Those who improve through audits may be those who are motivated to do so, thus are those with better performance to begin with, and therefore with least margin for improvement. Conversely, those who perform the worst may be the least motivated to change, short of coercion. Coercion (through withholding of payments, accreditation) has worked to improve performance in outright errors of care.

Chapter 11: Much must be done to improve patient behavior and compliance if the process of care is to have maximum effect on outcomes.

Experiences with Quality of Care Assessment and Assurance

Brook, R. H., and Appel, F. A. "Quality-of-Care Assessment: Choosing a Method for Peer Review." *New England Journal of Medicine* 288(1973) 1323–1329.

This classic study compares five current peer-review methods applied to the same charts of 296 patients with urinary tract infection, hypertension, or ulcers.

	% of 296 Patients Judged Receiving Adequate Care
1. Implicit review of process (was process likely to help in outcome?)	23
2. Implicit review of outcome (could it have been improved by better process?)	63
3. Implicit review of process and outcome combined (total statement of adequacy of care)	27
4. Explicit review of process (based on list of criteria)	1–2
5. Explicit review of outcome (based on list of criteria)	40–44

It is still unclear which method of assessment gives the most useful information, although the most common method is the most severe in judgment. It is also uncertain which exact processes of care are likely to lead to good outcomes for several common, non-trivial conditions.

Institute of Medicine. "Assessing Quality in Health Care: An Evaluation." Washington, D.C.: National Academy of Sciences, 1976.

This Institute of Medicine study reviewed 18 quality of care assessment programs (most in PSROs or large HMOs) regarded as "better programs." An arbitrary "ideal quality assurance system" was used for comparisons and has the following attributes:

1.   an organizational entity exists within a health center for the purpose of assessing quality;
2.   goals and criteria are established;
3.   an information system exists;
4.   a representative sample of patients for assessment is selected;
5.   results are provided to patients, providers, and funding agencies; and
6.   corrective actions are taken on the basis of audits.

Quality of care assessment programs reviewed did not meet these characteristics but focused narrowly on the medical care process. Especially lacking were assessments of the validity of the programs themselves or their cost effectiveness.

The 18 programs were characterized generally as:

1.   lacking measurable goals of care, therefore the magnitude of "improvement" was undecipherable;
2.   oriented to patients who come for care rather than at the population at large, thus blunting the issue of access to care;
3.   majorly concerned with the PSRO triad: cost containment (utilization review), medical care evaluations (retrospective client review), profile analysis (patterns of provider/client care review) with no integration of the findings;
4.   having difficulty finding appropriate topics and criteria for review; and
5.   having difficulty "closing the loop," that is, changing performance based on audit.

The study also reviewed "effectiveness" of the assurance programs:

1.   no proof provided that medical care evaluations improve care;
2.   utilization review effect on cost-containment was not well documented and too simplistic. Fixed hospital costs and costs of alternative care were not accounted for; claims review programs did not need to be linked to quality review programs to control claims; and
3.   costs of review varied widely.

It is unlikely that a single review program can cover cost, utilization and technical (medical) control. The study therefore recommends:

1.   Reviews should target "questionable patterns of care"—that is, identify truly inappropriate care, with more profiles of care to focus on errant providers.
2.   National experiments should be conducted to measure health status, utilization, and costs in regions with and without review mechanisms.
3.   More health care research should be organized. "Assessment of assessment" and research on short-term ("proximate") outcome measures are needed.
4.   Indices of quality—especially in areas of access—should be expanded.
5.   Assessment of chronic illness-care programs in terms of patient function is needed.
6.   Quality of care assessment should be expanded to involve consumers.
7.   Ways to convert the findings of assessments into changes in the behavior of providers and clients should be researched.

White, N. H.; Ryland, M. A.; Giebink, G. A.; and McConatha, D. *Ambulatory Care Quality Assurance Project: Volume I Development and Application of a Model.* DHEW, Public Health Service Health Services Administration, Bureau of Quality Assurance, USGPO Washington D.C., 1976.

A private consultant group reviewed on-going Quality of Medical Care Assurance Programs (QAP) of 27 large, well-known ambulatory health care centers (Kaiser Permanente, Harvard Community Health Plan, etc.). The planning and executing of nine components of an ideal QAP were first described and then each of the following components was scored at each of the sites:

1.   development of approach;
2.   establishment of administrative procedures;
3.   selection of topics and procedures for review;

4.   criteria development;
5.   identification of data elements and services;
6.   data collection and processing;
7.   review procedures;
8.   decision making and feedback; and
9.   evaluation, restudy and further action.
(Only the last 2 items can be called "Assurance.")

On a scale of 1.0, items 5, 6, and 3 achieved scores of 0.70, 0.73, and 0.80. Items 9 and 8 scored lowest: 0.26 and 0.40, respectively. All others rated about 0.5 to 0.6. These results show that while assessment is done regularly and easily, assurance is seldom done.

When scores were correlated to several program variables, suggestive relationships indicated that—
1.   a well-budgeted QAP scored higher; and
2.   sites getting data from claims forms scored higher.
     It was also discovered that
     a) most sites viewed QAP as a "project," not as an intrinsic operation;
     b) QAP was done for varied purposes such as cost-control, quality control, and research; and
     c) "Quality review was often viewed as a function that could be reduced or completely stopped for a time without having effect on the quality of services delivered."

Barnes, R. "Five Blocks to Medical Audit." In *The Changing Health Care Team: Improving Effectiveness in Patient Care*, edited by S. Zoog and S. Yarnall. Seattle, Washington: Medical Communications and Services Association, 1976.

The author identifies five reasons why medical audit is generally so unrewarding and ineffective:
1.   physician resistance to authority (especially governmental);
2.   lack of training for audit (and lack of even a simple set of credible rules for doing audit);
3.   use of "easy to live by" local criteria;

4.   reluctance to engage in peer review; and
5.   failure or inability to act on findings.

Report of the Joint National Committee on Detection, Evaluation, and Treatment of High Blood Pressure. DHEW, Public Health Service, National Institute of Health, Bethesda, Maryland, 1977.

There is an increasing use of specific minimum protocols of cost-effective treatment based on the stage of illness. Hypertension has the best developed protocol in the "stepped-care" approach. The way the criteria were developed is unique: a joint national committee, drawn from the American Academy of Family Physicians, American College of Cardiology, American College of Physicians, American Heart Association, American Medical Association, National Kidney Foundation, National Medical Association, U.S. Public Health Service, and Veterans Administration, met together and decided on standards.

Comment: Is this how national criteria will be set for all medical care under national health insurance?

Ridgway, V. F. "Dysfunctional Consequences of Performance Measurements." *Administrative Science Quarterly* 1(1956): 569–575.

This article discusses quantitative performance measurements:
1.   Single criteria are superficial and force direction of program activity, such as "productivity."
2.   Multiple measurements produce uncertainty over which criterion to pay attention to.
3.   Composite measurements which use an index blur individual components. Program managers demand an increase in composite "score" without a proportionate increase in resources. The use of an index may cause one to obey the "ratchet"

principle which makes each score the baseline for the next evaluation.

Comment: All measurements, even for information purposes, affect performance and not always positively, and the way information is gathered may distort original goals.

Koran, L. M. "The Reliability of Clinical Methods, Data and Judgments" (Two Parts). *The New England Journal of Medicine* 293 (1975): 642–646, and 293(1975): 695–701.

Contrary to its title, this article presents an excruciatingly detailed review of the unreliability of peer clinical judgments and data; even where two physicians agree on a particular observation, much of the agreement is due to chance alone.

Terminology, criteria, data forms must be agreed upon; all or none criteria should be used (such as present-absent, never-do-it, and always-do-it, in judging quality).

Spector, R.; McGrath, P.; Alpert, J.; Cohen, P.; and Aikins, H. "Medical Care by Nurses in an Internal Medicine Clinic." *Journal of the American Medical Association* 232(1975): 1234–1237.

One effect of audit is to raise costs. For example: a study of nurse practitioners in a University-Hospital medical clinic showed adequate performance compared to physicians. However, excessive cautiousness by the nurses, increasing visits, and physician consultations created a higher cost. The cautiousness was attributed at least in part to the audit itself.

Zusman, J. "Can Program Evaluation Be Saved from Its Enthusiasts?" *American Journal of Psychiatry* 133(1976): 1300–1305.

Program outcome evaluation (here in mental health programs) seldom does much good for the following reasons:

1.   The results are accepted or not according to professional, political, or consumer group biases and pressures (even to the point of loading the dice for or against the outcome of the evaluation).
2.   They are often too technical in content or the findings are easily attacked or reinterpreted by critics.
3.   The data are often not used to make changes in programs, especially if there are no political or other strong incentives to do so.

An appropriate evaluation ought to have the chance of making a difference to a program. Pilot in-depth research studies should be done on prototypic programs. For the operations of most programs, the evaluation should be done against operational goals with either the operations or the goals changed as necessary. For example, a suicide-prevention center has little impact on suicide rates; actual practice may call for change in goals such as becoming a crisis-counseling center.

Bailar, J. C., III. "Clinical Biostatistics." *Clinical Pharmacology and Therapeutics* 20(1976): 113–119.

Bailar's laws of data analysis can, with slight translation, be applied to quality of care assessment:

1.   There are no "right" answers; several explanations fit the same available data, some more perfectly.
2.   Statistics (assessment, audits, explicit criteria) are not the only way to wisdom; direct observations (the clinical approach) are also important.
3.   Rare events do happen.
4.   Do not accumulate masses of data in hopes of finding one flake of gold. Simplify, direct and structure an investigation; anchor it to specific goals.
5.   It is easier to get in than get out of complex statistics and audits.

6. No sample is ever big enough. Use only enough to tell you about changes in organization and management, unless you are doing research.

7. Know if you are committing statistical hanky panky—such as, assessing easy conditions or hypertension only.

8. More quacks practice statistics (quality of care assessment) than medicine.

9. Good work takes time.

10. No analysis is ever perfect.

11. Something is always wrong with the data—records, entries, surveys.

12. Politics and emotion generally take over from logic.

Studies of Medical Care

Practice Profile

"Ambulatory Medical Care Rendered in Physicians' Offices—United States, 1975." *Advance Data from Vital and Health Statistics of the National Center for Health Statistics.* U.S. Department of Health, Education and Welfare, 1977. October 12.

Over three-fourths of health care in the U.S. is provided in private physicians' offices. The following data describe those practices.

1. Number of visits —nearly 600,000,000
2. % of visits to FPs & GPs —40%
3. Visits per person —2.7
   - per age <15 —1.9
   - per age >65 —4.3
   - per sex —female 3.2, male 2.2
   - per color —white 2.8, other 2.2
4. Diagnosis (% of visits)
   - acute: chronic —55:45
   - 5 major groups:
     - well —18%
     - respiratory —14%
     - circulatory —10%
     - nervous & sensory — 8%
     - accidents, poisoning & violence — 7%

       _____

       57% of total
5. Seriousness (% of visits)
   - not serious —49%
   - slightly serious —32%
   - serious —19% (29% in elderly)
6. Therapy (% of visits)
   - drugs —44%
   - counseling —20%
7. Duration of visit (% of visits)
   - 15 minutes —76%
   - 30 minutes — 6%

Rogers, D. E. "The Challenge of Primary Care." *Daedalus* 106 (1977): 81–103.

This article reveals patterns of physical, social, and psychological problems in a hypothetical private general practice. These patterns are probably consistent within many areas of the United States.

In an average general practice, 77% of the consultations are for minor illnesses, 4% for life threatening episodes, and 19% for chronic conditions. By functional class, 41% of the consultations are for respiratory disease, 17% for psychological conditions.

Brown, J. W.; Robertson, L. S.; Kosa J.; and Alpert, J. J. "A Study of General Practice in Massachusetts." *Journal of the American Medical Association* 216(1971): 301–306.

A review of 12,835 visits to 15 Massachusetts general private practitioners showed that 25% of all patients had no disease, 48% had acute symptoms, and 56% came for follow-up.

Bellin, S. S.; Locke, B. Z.; and New, M. "The Neighborhood Health Center a a Mental Health Diagnostic Service." *Public Health Reports* 91(1976): 446–451.

In a neighborhood health center serving an indigent ghetto community, the annual prevalence of psychiatric diagnoses was 10% (20% in those over 40). This figure is probably an underestimate of the true figure for the community.

Stewart, M. M. "Primary Care in Urban Hospitals." *Bulletin of the New York Academy of Medicine* 53(1977): 83–102.

FREQUENCY OF PRESENTING PROBLEMS AT
AN ADULT WALK-IN CLINIC AT A LARGE CITY HOSPITAL

Problem	% of Total	Cumulative Frequency [%]
Gastrointestinal	9.6	
Skin	9.1	
Joint pain	8.1	
Renewal of prescription	7.7	
Back pain	6.1	40.6
Sore throat	5.1	
Emotional	4.4	
Genitourinary or venereal disease	4.1	
Cough	4.1	
Hypertension	4.0	62.3
Headache	3.7	
Ear	3.3	
Chest wall pain	3.0	
Upper respiratory infection	2.7	75.0
Gynecology	2.6	
All other	22.4	
Total	100.0	

(n=1,850 patients, 2,131 complaints)

Cooper, T. "Infectious Disease: No Cause for Complacency." *The Journal of Infectious Diseases* 134(1976): 510–512.

    The return or nondisappearance of infectious diseases is a major U.S. medical problem. They are therefore a good topic for an audit of prevention and care. The following diseases are considered in this article: influenza, venereal disease (especially gonorrhea, genital herpes, chlamydial urethritis in men), scabies (nearly one million cases in 1974), viral hepatitis, tuberculosis (especially in high-risk groups), meningitis (in children), urinary tract infections, gram negative infections (in compromised patients), and travelers' diarrhea.

Process to Outcome Links

HYPERTENSION

1) **Knox, R. A., and Black, H.** "Deaths from Heart Disease on Decline." *The Boston Globe*, October 30, 1977; 2) **Knox, R. A.** "Heart Death Decline Baffles Medicine." *The Boston Globe*, October 31, 1977; 3) **Martin, S. P., Donaldson, M. C., London, D. C., Peterson, O. L., and Colton, T.** "Inputs into Coronary Care During 30 Years. A Cost-Effectiveness Study." *Annals of Internal Medicine* 81(1976): 289–293; and 4) **Hyman, E. S.** "Death Rates and Digoxin." *Medical World News*, Vol. 19, March 6, 1978, pp. 119–120.

Cardiovascular disease (principally heart attacks and stroke) is still America's number one cause of death, killing nearly one million persons annually. The rate of fatal coronaries had risen 20% between 1950 and the mid-1960s. In a startling reversal, deaths from heart attacks and stroke have fallen 20% between 1968 and 1975, with a greater rate of decline between 1973 and 1975. Additionally, death rates attributed directly to hypertension fell 45% in the same period.

The decline is seen in all age groups, both sexes, whites, and blacks. Using 1965 death rates, the number who died of cardiovascular disease in 1975 were 220,000 fewer than expected.

Comment: Coronary vascular disease is common; its epidemiology, biology, biochemistry, and treatment are as well known as for any disease. Although enormous quantities of money go toward research and therapy for this disease, the causes of its decline as well as its future directions are unknown. Consider the following approaches, all of which could have contributed to its decline:

1. Hypertension Control—A health education and primary care approach. In 1971, 37% of hypertensives were aware of and getting some treatment for their condition; in 1977 the figure was 48%.

2. Diet—A health education and public policy approach. Since 1964, per capita consumption of milk and cream fell 19%,

butter 32%, eggs 13%, animal fats 57%, while consumption of unsaturated fats increased by 44%.

3. Smoking—A health education and public policy approach. The Surgeon General's report on smoking was issued in 1964. Since then a smaller proportion of Americans smoke, and those who do, mostly use some form of filtered or reduced tar-nicotine brands.

4. Exercise—A health education and public policy approach. Eleven percent of American males now claim to jog or run regularly. Since President Kennedy established the President's Council on Physical Fitness, numerous community and school-based athletic and exercise programs have started.

5. Drug Use—A public policy approach. An intriguing argument is presented that digitalis intoxication could have accounted for 35,000 to 50,000 deaths per year. Poorly standardized digoxin may have put patients at a 10% risk of intoxication with each refill. In 1974, digoxin was restandardized; the accelerating decline in death rates since 1975 could substantially reflect this simple but potent change.

6. Improved Medical and Surgical Therapy—A medical technology approach. Cardiopulmonary resuscitation, coronary by-pass surgery, use of propranolol, and coronary care units have all been suggested as major determinants in the decline of deaths from cardiovascular disease. The article by Martin et al., however, does not document any significant changes in either in-hospital mortality or in the duration of stay between 1939 and 1969 despite marked increases in diagnostic tests and treatments. A small change between 1939 and 1949 arose from antibiotic treatment of complicating pneumonia.

Should funds now go to research in and application of medical technology, or to community-based programs and health education? How vigorous should public policy interventions become?

Veterans Administration Cooperative Study Group on Antihypertensive Agents. "Effects of Treatment on Morbidity in Hypertension. Results in Patients with Diastolic Blood Pressures Averaging

115 Through 129 mm Hg." *Journal of the American Medical Association* 202(1967): 116–122.

One hundred forty-three male patients (77 black) with hypertension (diastolic pressures 115 to 129 mm Hg) were randomly assigned to one of two groups. The first group, composed of 73 patients, received three active drugs—thiazide, resperine, and hydralazine. The second group, composed of 70 patients, received placebos. Both groups were followed for 16 to 21 months. Compliance was high as there was only an 8% dropout rate. The treatment group had two untoward events and no deaths (3% attack rate); the placebo group had 27 complicating events with four deaths (39% attack rate)—a 13-fold difference.

The 29 events included: 10 retinal hemorrhages, 5 strokes or transient ischemia, 3 aortic tears or rupture (all died), 3 BP out of control, 2 deterioration of kidney function, 1 drug toxicity, and 1 unknown cause of death.

Veterans Administration Cooperative Study Group on Antihypertensive Agents. "Effects of Treatment on Morbidity in Hypertension, II. Results in Patients with Diastolic Blood Pressure Averaging 90 Through 114 mm Hg." *Journal of the American Medical Association* 213(1970): 1143–1152.

Three hundred eighty male patients (158 black) with moderate hypertension were assigned either to an active treatment group (186 patients) or to a placebo group (194 patients), and followed for nearly four years on the average.

Thirty-five major morbid events occurred in the placebo group (18% attack rate) compared to nine in the treatment group (5% attack rate)—a four-fold difference. Twenty placebo group patients developed more severe hypertension as well. Nineteen deaths occurred in the placebo group and eight in the control group. The cumulative incidence rate for all adverse events was 55% in the control group compared to 18% in the study group—a three-fold difference.

Benefit correlated with the initial severity of pressure. The protection was limited to prevention of stroke, congestive failure, renal damage, and accelerated hypertension rather than coronary artery disease. Treated diastolic pressures fell to an average of 17 mm Hg, and rose 1 mm Hg in the placebo group.

Freis, E. D. "How Far Should Blood Pressure Be Lowered in Treating Hypertension?" *Journal of the American Medical Association* 232(1975): 1017–1018.

In Denmark, no differences in mortality or organ damage were found between hypertensives whose blood pressures were reduced to normal and those whose pressures fell only part way to normal. Support for this finding comes from the well-known Veterans Administration which showed:

CARDIOVASCULAR COMPLICATIONS

Control of BP	(% in 3 Years)	
None	29%	
Poor	15%	} not significant statistically
Good	10%	

It may not be necessary, in all cases, to force blood pressure to "normal."

Nobrega, F. T.; Morrow, G. W., Jr.; Smoldt, R. K.; and Offord, K. P. "Quality Assessment in Hypertension: Analysis of Process and Outcome Methods." *The New England Journal of Medicine* 296(1977): 145–148.

One hundred thirty-eight patients with hypertension (diastolic over 95 mm Hg on three or more visits) followed at the Mayo Clinic with comparable duration of illness (1965–1970) were followed up in 1974. Criteria for process of care were developed by two specialist and three generalist internists. Six categories of process included history (23 items), physical (26 items), initial lab tests (13 items), special diagnostics (9 items), treatment (8 items) and follow-up (10 items)—a total of 89 process bits.

In a review of the 138 charts for completeness of *process*, the following was found:

	% of Charts Incomplete
history	49%
physical	43%
initial lab	25%
special diagnosis	30%
treatment	21%
follow-up	86%

The higher the level of initial blood pressure, the more complete the process. Patient compliance was high; 130/138 took medication faithfully.

In review of their outcome:

8/138 died, all over 70 years of age.

Initial Diastolic BP (mm Hg):	<104	<119	>120
Follow-up:			
% Diastolic <90	70	65	50
Deaths	1	5	2

Process to Outcome Links:

 # With Outcome Diastolic BP:

% process items complete	<90 (good)	91–100 (fair)	>100 or death (poor)
>67%	27	14	5
33–66%	24	13	9
<33%	31	7	8

In an analysis of the six process categories independently compared to outcome levels, essentially no significant link was found.

In an analysis of all patient and provider related items compared to outcome (diastolic BP) only patient weight, age, initial pressure and specific therapy were significantly related. Patient satisfaction, intensity of follow-up, process items, and cost-convenience factors were not related.

The authors conclude:

1. Physicians do not follow their own long lists of criteria too well.
2. Outcomes of care were generally good, nonetheless.
3. Except for diagnosis (a recognition of the problem) and specific treatment, little else matters in the process of care.

The Johns Hopkins University EMCRO. "Review of Care for Hypertension." Unpublished, 1975.

In 25 hypertensives, process audit showed:

Patients getting optimal or adequate care			12 (48%)
Patients getting inadequate care			13 (52%)

		OUTCOMES (BP control):	
		Good	Poor
PROCESS:	Optimal/Adequate	58%	42%
	Inadequate	23%	77%

While optimal or adequate care doubles good outcomes, it is only effective in half the number of given cases.

Brook, R. H., and Davies-Avery, A. "Quality Assurance and Cost Control in Ambulatory Care." Santa Monica, Calif.: The Rand Corporation, 1977.

In a monograph on cost-control and quality assurance, the authors show how "improving quality" by adherence to explicit process criteria would markedly increase ambulatory care costs. If all sore throats, for example, were treated by ideal standards, the annual cost of therapy for this illness alone would be four billion dollars.

There is much waste in medical care due to: 1. aberrant life-styles, 2. noncompliance, 3. failure of follow-up, and 4. only a small positive effect of process on outcome.

For high blood pressure, Brook shows the following outcomes, from his own clinical study:

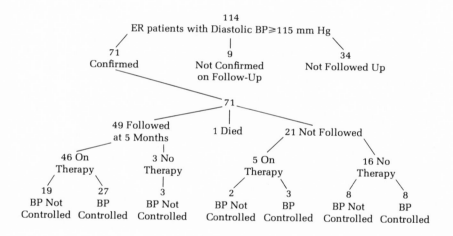

$$\frac{\text{Control}}{\text{No Control}}\text{---on Therapy} = 30/51 \qquad 59\%$$

$$\frac{\text{Control}}{\text{No Control}}\text{---off Therapy} = 8/19 \qquad 42\%$$

Chi$-^2$ = 0.96
  Not significant

Sackett, D. L.; Taylor, D. W.; Haynes, R. B.; Gibson, E. S.; Roberts, R. S.; and Johnson, A. L. "The Short-Term Disadvantages of Being Diagnosed Hypertensive." *Clinical Research* 25(1977): 266A.

Diagnosis and the start of treatment of hypertensive steel workers were associated with a dramatic increase in absenteeism compared with hypertensives unaware of their condition.

Haynes, R. B.; Sackett, D. L.; Gibson, E. S.; Taylor, D. W.; Hackett, B. C.; Roberts, R. S.; and Johnson, A. L. "Improvement of Medication Compliance in Uncontrolled Hypertension." *Lancet* 2(1976): 1265–1268.

Thirty-eight previously noncompliant hypertensive men whose pressures remained high were given standard care or a marked increase in attention.

(Compliance—Taking 80% or more of drug):

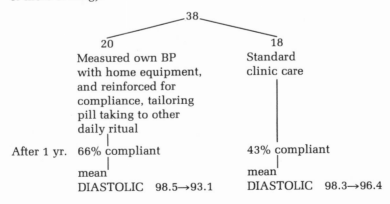

	20	18
	Measured own BP with home equipment, and reinforced for compliance, tailoring pill taking to other daily ritual	Standard clinic care
After 1 yr.	66% compliant	43% compliant
	mean DIASTOLIC 98.5→93.1	mean DIASTOLIC 98.3→96.4

Redman, C. W. G.; Beilin, L. J.; Bonnar, J.; and Ounsted, M. K. "Fetal Outcome in Trial of Antihypertensive Treatment in Pregnancy." *Lancet* 2(1976): 754–756.

Treatment for moderate hypertension in a particular high risk group—pregnant women—was associated with improved fetal outcome.

Control
116
|
fetal loss: 9

Treated (alpha methyldopa)
116
|
fetal loss: 1

$p < 0.05$

URINARY TRACT INFECTION

Brook, R. H., and Appel, F. A. "Quality-of-Care Assessment: Choosing a Method for Peer Review." *The New England Journal of Medicine* 288(1973): 1323–1329.

In a review of several methods to assess adequacy of care, outcomes were given for urinary tract infection:

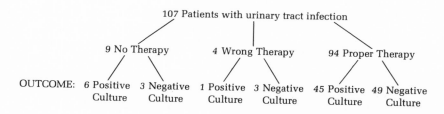

107 Patients with urinary tract infection

9 No Therapy   4 Wrong Therapy   94 Proper Therapy

OUTCOME: 6 Positive   3 Negative   1 Positive   3 Negative   45 Positive   49 Negative
Culture   Culture   Culture   Culture   Culture   Culture

The results show that: Of 13 patients not receiving therapy or being given improper treatments, 6 (46%) improved (they had a negative culture); of 94 given proper care, 49 (52%) improved.

Rubenstein, L.; Mates, S.; and Sidel, V. W. "Quality-of-Care Assessment By Process and Outcome Scoring. Use of Weighted Algorithmic Assessment Criteria for Evaluation of Emergency Room Care of Women with Symptoms of Urinary Tract Infection." *Annals of Internal Medicine* 86(1977): 617−625.

The quality of care of urinary tract infections in 165 patients at two hospital OPDs was assessed by matching process criteria (Physician Performance Index) and outcome criteria (satisfaction, persistence of symptoms, understanding of illness and treatment). The scores were distributed around several criteria weighted for importance.

Process Criteria	Max Points	Outcome Criteria	Max Points
History (13 items)	25	Satisfaction	
Physical Exam (6 items)	14	with system	2
Appropriate Lab Tests (2 items)	7	with provider	2
Appropriate Treatment	8	Symptoms	3
Follow-up	4	Knowledge	3
Physician Performance Index	58	Outcome Index	10

Process audit required extensive records search; outcome audit required telephone follow-ups (48% of sample).

The findings were:

1. Mean process score (Physician Performance Index) was 30 (only 16/165 scores were over 40).
2. Satisfaction, understanding, and feeling better were present in over half the patients (Outcome Index average about 7).
3. Correlation of process score to outcome score was present but weak ($r = 0.379$).
4. For process scores under 20, all patients had a poor outcome score (less than 5 out of 10).
5. For process scores over 35, all patients had a good outcome score (over 5 out of 10).
6.

Mean Process Score		Mean Outcome Score
<20	("poor care")	3.4
20−34	("intermediate care")	7.0
>34	("excellent care")	7.4

7.   Good outcomes were highly correlated with being given anti-
     microbials appropriately.
8.   Actual outcomes—cure of urinary infection—was not fol-
     lowed up. But a high percentage of cases remit spontane-
     ously.
     The major conclusion is that medical care processes can most
improve outcomes by moving from "poor" to "adequate" care; but
they cannot do much more in moving to "optimal" care, which is
likely to raise costs unacceptably.

Daschner, F., and Marget, W. "Treatment of Recurrent Urinary
Tract Infection in Children. II. Compliance of Parents and Children
with Antibiotic Therapy Regimen." *Acta Paediatrica Scandinavica*
64(1975): 105–108.

Of 93 children with recurrent UTI:

Took Drug	Infection Rate/Year	
Faithfully: 32%	3.9	
Irregularly: 49%	4.8	Significant Difference
Not At All: 19%	7.2	

Even irregular compliance had the same effect as faithful
compliance; outcomes were improved by 46% over no treatment at
all.

ASSORTED COMMON ILLNESSES

Brook, R. H.; Berg, N. H.; and Schecter, P. A. "Effectiveness of
Nonemergency Care via an Emergency Room: A Study of 166 patients with Gastrointestinal Symptoms." *Annals of Internal Medicine* 78(1973): 329–333.

This study is of 166 patients who went to a university-community hospital emergency room with GI symptoms. The quality of care was measured by a single process criterion ("Treat if x-ray abnormal") and by a single outcome criterion ("Asymptomatic and good life-activity or same/worse with decreased activity"). One hundred fifty-seven patients were followed up.

	Outcome:		
Process:	**Good**	**Not Good**	**Ratio, Good:Not Good**
Adequate	30	54	.56
Inadequate	23	50	.46
	53	104	

The study shows that a sample process criterion had no effect on outcome because while 68% of patients had normal x-rays, ¾ of these patients remained symptomatic. Only 23 patients of the original 166 (14% overall) ever got any treatment which means that a substantial number with good outcomes got better without treatment, and a substantial number with poor outcomes might have gotten better with treatment, both regardless of x-ray. The cost per patient averaged $313.

"A system that deemphasizes diagnosis and simply treats patients with subacute or chronic gastrointestinal symptoms with drugs or reassurance, without performing many diagnostic tests, might produce better patient outcome and also be less expensive . . . Additional minimal expenditures on follow-up efforts might substantially improve patient outcome."

Starfield, B., and Scheff, D. "Effectiveness of Pediatric Care: The Relationship Between Processes and Outcome." *Pediatrics* 49(1972): 547–552.

Of 53 children with anemia:

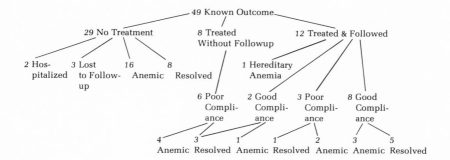

1. 27% got well without treatment;
2. 45% got well with treatment;
3. 33% got well with poor compliance; and
4. 50% got well with good compliance.

The key finding is that treatment, follow-up, and good compliance occurred in only 16% of patients, but even in this group only half got better, while 27% got better with no treatment at all.

Comment: This finding is surprising in view of the supposed ease and efficacy of treatment for a common condition.

Brook, R. H.; Appel, F. A.; Avery, C.; Orman, M.; and Stevenson, R. "Effectiveness of Inpatient Follow-up Care." *The New England Journal of Medicine* 285(1971): 1509–1513.

This study directly links process of care to outcome for a condition whose outcome is soon known ("proximate-outcome"). The condition is a person's functional capacity six months after discharge from the hospital. Criteria for good process were:

1. if the patient was referred to a hospital clinic and kept 50% of the appointments;
2. if the patient was referred to an outside physician, and then seen at least once;

3.   if the patient was discharged on drugs for a major condition, and then compliant with physician orders; and

4.   if the patient had a chronic condition, and then a source of continuing care was designated.

Criteria of the outcome were functional:

	Level I	Level II	Level III
Symptoms:	Few or none	NOT	Worse or dead
Major Activity Status:	Ok, and with good ambulation	I	Worse or dead
		OR	
Ambulatory Function:	No impairment or slight impairment	III	Worse or dead

RESULTS OF FOLLOW-UP

502 Consecutive City Hospital Admissions

403 Discharged   53 to Chronic Hospital

At 6 Months: 363 Alive   40 Died   29 Alive   24 Died

STUDY OF MEDICAL CARE—PROCESS TO OUTCOME LINKS
(Implicit Review)

Outcome:

Process:		Level I	Level II	Level III	Inadequate Data
	Good	157	65	41	2
	Poor	36	40	32	12
	Inadequate Data	—	—	9	9

One hundred fifty-seven patients had good outcomes and good processes. Seventy-two had poor processes and poor outcomes (Levels II and III, 40 + 32); but of those with poor outcomes only 39 were causally linked to process (implicit judgment).

Comment: For a complete analysis, one would really need to know the proportion of good outcomes with good processes which would have been good anyway. Since 36/193 (19%) of those with good outcomes had poor processes, we might guess that a like proportion of those with good outcomes and good processes (30/157) were independent of process. This leads to the following analysis:

OUTCOMES:	Poor, Directly Related to Process	Poor, Unrelated to Process	Good, Directly Related to Process	Good, Unrelated to Process
POOR PROCESS	39	33	0*	36
GOOD PROCESS	0+	106	127	30

+unlikely
*impossible

1. 120/403 patients had poor process, or 30%. This is a measure of PROCESS QUALITY.
2. 39/403 patients had poor outcomes directly related to poor process, or 10%. This is a measure of ADDITIONAL CONTROLLABLE QUALITY.
3. 127/403 patients had good outcomes related to good process, or 32%. This is a measure of QUALITY TO BE MAINTAINED.

Sanazaro, P. J., and Worth, R. M. "Concurrent Quality Assurance in Hospital Care Report of a Study by Private Initiative in PSRO." *New England Journal of Medicine* 298(1978): 1171–1177.

Adherence to essential criteria of care was not significantly related to better outcomes except for acute myocardial infarction and bacterial pneumonia.

This study compared 24 experimental and 26 control hospitals, with 5,604 cases of seven conditions—acute myocardial infarction, bacterial pneumonia, urinary tract infection, gastroenteritis, upper GI bleeding, appendicitis, and cholecystitis. The audits were conducted in five PSRO areas, incorporating concurrent quality assurance (CQA) into utilization reviews. The presence of CQA in a hospital had only a slight effect on overall physician adherence to the criteria. The cost of administering CQA was $1.23 per patient.

Coltin, K. L.; Neisuler, R.; and Lurie, R. S. *"Evaluation of a Program To Facilitate the Integration of a Low-Income Population into a Prepaid Group Practice Plan."* Boston: Harvard Community Health Plan, 1976.

Harvard Community Health Plan (HCHP) is a large, pre-paid group practice. The majority of members have been insured through various Boston and Cambridge-based employers. A minority of members are medicaid-eligible or "near poor" working class whose premiums are subsidized by the federal government. As part of an evaluation of the Quality of Care delivered to the three groups (Employer, Medicaid, "Near poor"), process and outcome were measured simultaneously for several indicator conditions.

Obesity (289 cases)		Hypertension (41 cases)		Anemia (252 cases)	
Treated	17%	Tested	73%	*Treated*	45%
Improved*	39%	Treated	54%	Improved*	46%
Unimproved	61%	Improved*	29%	Unimproved	54%
Untreated	83%			*Untreated*	55%
Improved	36%			Improved	33%
Unimproved	64%			Unimproved	67%
*(weight reduction 5% or more)		*(Diastolic BP < 90 mm Hg at all times in one year)		*(Hgb > 12 gm%)	

Berenson, R.; Bohrer, R.; and White, W. Analysis of Quality, Productivity, and Cost in Community Health Centers. Presented at the

Annual meeting of the American Public Health Association, November 1975, Chicago, Ill.

Data from 92 of over 200 CHCs were analyzed along the following indices:

1. center attributes (area of nation, size, experience, urban or rural location);
2. measures of provider productivity;
3. measures of cost;
4. measures of client utilization;
5. staffing patterns; and
6. "Quality of Care" as measured by external (Drew & Morehead) audits of the total center organization and performance.

The results showed:

1. no correlation between "quality" and utilization, staffing pattern, or productivity;
2. a positive correlation between "quality" and cost;
3. bringing people to the center (*access*) increased productivity, but increasing social services (*availability*) increased cost;
4. increasing the number of elderly patients decreased physician productivity; and
5. center attributes did not correlate with cost, productivity, or quality.

The obvious conclusions are a) that "quality," especially increased social services and care for the elderly, are going to increase costs, and b) that generic considerations of "quality" and organization of care are independent of the structural features and maturity of a health center.

Mushlin, A. I.; Appel, F. A.; Pozen, J. T.; Zauber, A. G.; and Koch, J. F. "The Use of Patient-Reported Problem Status in Evaluating Ambulatory Care." Johns Hopkins Health Services Research and Development Center. Presented at the National Meeting of the American Federation for Clinical Research, 3 May 1975, in Atlantic City, New Jersey.

This study documents outcome status as reported by the patient for a specific problem in terms of frequency and intensity of symptoms, degree of activity limitation, and anxiety, which are all tested initially and one month later. This technique requires a high degree of follow-up and client compliance. Three conditions that are studied are viral sore throat (VST), upper respiratory infection (URI), and urinary tract infection (UTI). Outcome criteria: After one month, the patient should report no symptoms, no limitation of activity, and no anxiety.

	VST	URI	UTI
% Not meeting outcome criteria:	8%	32%	25%

Thirty-five percent of those not meeting criteria had comorbid or relevant factors that could complicate outcomes (against 9% of those who did meet criteria).

The proportion of patients with inadequate diagnostic work-up or inadequate treatment was the same in the groups with good or bad outcomes. Initial diagnosis was more often incorrect (25% vs. 3% of cases; 1 vs. 5) in the poor outcome group. However, most of the misdiagnoses were for mononucleosis which has its own course whether diagnosed or not.

By implicit review:

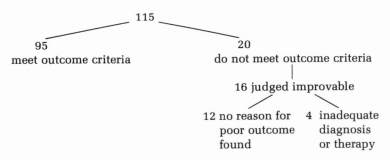

Comment: VST and URI are generally trivial, self-limited conditions; by the nature of the follow-up, an artificially high degree of patient complaints or anxiety may have been fostered. Where patient reported outcomes were unsatisfactory, most have nothing to do with the process of care.

Payne, B. C. "Outcome Study." In *The Quality of Medical Care: Evaluation and Improvement.* Chicago, Illinois: Hospital Research and Educational Trust, 1976.

The authors have constructed a Physician Performance Index (PPI) based on a series of process criteria, such as history taking, physical exam, use of diagnostic tests, special procedures and therapy. They correlate the PPI with the patients' outcomes (intermediate or final) in 24 major medical conditions. Positive correlations were statistically significant at $P<0.02$ in only two conditions (subsidence of diarrhea in children and survival from breast cancer), and $P<0.05$ in four other conditions (lack of postoperative edema, or recurrence in breast cancer, survival from cervical cancer, or clearing of chronic urinary infection). The study indicates tenuous process to outcome links for most conditions.

Increasing the PPI from the ambulatory care level of 45% to that of modal specialists (78%) would increase costs of care by over 140%.

Dutton, C. B.; Hoffman, S.; Ryan, L. K.; and Ward, T. J. "Ambulatory Health Care: Medical Audit System." *New York State Journal of Medicine* 74(1974): 1545–1550.

At the Whitney M. Young Neighborhood Health Center, a problem-oriented audit was designed to evaluate the process of medical care according to predefined standards. Protocols designed by center physicians for diagnostic evaluation and treatment were already used by providers. An audit form was designed to collect data on four health problems. The audit assessed provider compliance with protocols.

The pediatric otitis media audit evaluated treatment, follow-up, and clinical outcome according to explicit criteria. Forty-nine episodes were reviewed: therapy was found appropriate in all cases; 34 cases were resolved, 3 unresolved, and 12 had indeterminate outcomes. The result was 69% good outcome with good process.

An adult hypertension audit evaluated initial diagnosis, follow-up, and outcome. Of 34 cases, 9 were lost to follow-up; of the remaining 25, hypertension was controlled in 10. The result was 40% good outcome with process unspecified.

An adult urinary tract infection audit assessed diagnosis, treatment, follow-up and outcome according to explicit criteria. In 45 cases: 20 had complete diagnosis; 41 received appropriate treatment; of the 39 episodes audited for follow-up, 10 were resolved. The result was 25% good outcome with good process.

Fifty-one cases of pediatric anemia were audited: of the 18 which met criteria for iron-deficiency anemia, 14 were treated and none had resolved outcomes. The result was 0% good outcome with good process.

Comment: The link between process and outcome is not established here as the outcome for those patients with poor process is not known, and a certain percent of those with good outcome would have gotten better anyway. However, at a maximum, the outcome of four common tracer conditions, where process was satisfactory, ranged from 0 to 69% satisfactory, showing a differential effect of process on particular diseases.

Fessel, W. J., and Van Brunt, E. E. "Assessing Quality of Care from the Medical Record." *The New England Journal of Medicine* 286(1972): 134–138.

In light of the criticisms which can be made of the medical record audit, studies were conducted in three hospitals to determine the relationship, if any, between the recorded processes of medical care and the outcome of that care. Information was abstracted from patients' records by a medical record librarian; her accuracy was checked and a 2.4% error rate found.

Fifty charts of appendectomy patients in each hospital were audited for eight commonly sought signs or symptoms. Although a significant disparity was found in the data from hospital to hospital, patient outcomes were the same in all three hospitals.

Fifty records of patients with acute myocardial infarction were studied from one hospital and were audited by two sets of criteria: 1. a process list of 44 items; and 2. a process list of 10 items found in previous studies to be related to survival or death. Two additional sets of 50 charts (one set = survived and uncomplicated; one set = died) were audited by a list of 26 explicit process criteria drawn up by three hospital cardiologists. As with appendectomy, no significant relation existed between the audit scores and any of the post-hospital outcomes for myocardial infarction.

These findings show that neither quality nor quantity of recorded data were related to outcomes for either of the two conditions. The authors conclude that chart audits do not reflect standards of care nor do explicit lists of process criteria relate to outcomes.

Kane, R. L.; Gardner, J.; Wright, D. D.; Snell, G.; Sundwall, D.; and Woolley, F. R. "Relationship between Process and Outcome in Ambulatory Care." *Medical Care* 15(1977): 961–965.

Four hundred ten new episodes of seven conditions treated by two family practices at the University of Utah Family Practice Residency program were reviewed for adequacy of process and outcome. The conditions were: otitis media, hypertension, bronchitis, pharyngitis, tonsilitis, urinary tract infection, and vaginitis. The process criteria reviewed were based either on PSRO explicit criteria (251 cases), or implicit judgment by supervisory physicians (162 cases).

The outcome criteria included a seven-step functional measure (from full activities without symptoms to death), or measures of patient satisfaction with care and outcome.

The results are:

		Functional Outcome:				
a.	Explicit process criteria, % adequate:	*Good*		*Poor*		
		81%		74%		
		Not significantly different				

		Functional Outcome:		Satisfaction:			
b.	Implicit process	*Good*	*Poor*	*with care*		*with outcome*	
	criteria, overall			*yes*	*no*	*yes*	*no*
	rating score	3.1	2.8	3.0	2.8	3.0	2.8
	(0=unacceptable,	Borderline					
	4=excellent)	Significance					

Comment: The relationships of good or poor process (implicitly or explicitly defined) to outcome (medically based, or client-reported) are virtually indistinguishable even in a generous sample of cases.

Moore, M.; Merson, M. H.; Charache, P.; and Shepard, R. H. "The Characteristics and Mortality of Outpatient-Acquired Pneumonia." *The Johns Hopkins Medical Journal* 140(1977): 9–14.

This article shows a remarkably low death rate from pneumonia (6%) even in a population previously known to have high death rates due to alcoholism, chronic complicating illnesses, recurrent illnesses, and undernutrition. The low death rate was attributed to the use of a single effective antibiotic; most patients received a type of penicillin.

Taylor, C., and Onion, D. K. "The First Six Months After Otitis Media." *The Journal of the Maine Medical Association* 66(1975): 280–281.

Ninety-eight percent of 89 children with otitis media recovered within three weeks of therapy. Although males had more recurrences than females, one-third of all the patients had a recurrence within six months. Compliance in taking medicines did not protect any patients from recurrence.

Hampton, J. R.; Harrison, M. J. G.; Mitchell, J. R. A.; and Seymour, C. "Relative Contributions of History-taking, Physical Examination and Laboratory Investigation to Diagnosis and Management of Medical Outpatients." *British Medical Journal* 2(1975): 486–489.

Of 80 new patients the initial diagnosis was the same as the final accepted diagnosis in 66 on the basis of a good history alone (83%).

The physical exam and laboratory tests gave the proper diagnosis in an additional seven each.

NURSE VS. PHYSICIAN CARE

Sackett, D. L.; Spitzer, W. O.; Gent, M.; and Roberts, R. S. "The Burlington Randomized Trial of the Nurse Practitioner: Health Outcomes of Patients." *Annals of Internal Medicine* 80(1974): 137–142.

Outcome measures were applied to primary care patients randomly allocated either to a family physician (FP) or a nurse practitioner (NP). The experiment lasted one year.

	MEASURE	FP	NP
A.	Mortality, per thousand	6.0	2.7
B.	Physical function: $\dfrac{\text{Before}}{\text{After}}$ Visit		
	1. % unimpaired mobility, vision, hearing	$\dfrac{50}{55}$	$\dfrac{45}{44}$
	2. % unimpaired daily activities	$\dfrac{82}{87}$	$\dfrac{77}{79}$
	3. Free from bed disability	$\dfrac{74}{75}$	$\dfrac{70}{76}$
C.	Emotional function 0.0 = poor 1.0 = good By standardized index	0.58	0.58
D.	Social function 0.0 = poor 1.0 = good By standardized index	0.83	0.84

Comment: Besides displaying equivalence of family physicians and nurse practitioners in patient outcomes, these figures show relatively small changes in physical functions over a year of medical care.

Lewis, C. E.; Resnik, B. A.; Schmidt, G.; and Waxman, D. "Activities, Events, and Outcomes in Ambulatory Patient Care." *The New England Journal of Medicine* 280(1969): 645–649.

The "Critical Incidents" technique was used to compare two medical practices—one by two nurse practitioners and the other by a physician. Adopting the classifications formulated in an earlier study, the authors evaluated the health providers according to the following categories: General Care, General Evaluation, Specific Evaluation, General Treatment, and Specific Treatment, in addition to 35 subcategories.

The study revealed that physicians did more technically oriented activities than nurses. However, both groups complemented each other in offering psychological and social support and organizing health care activities. Patients with five conditions were studied: hypertension, heart disease, obesity, depression, arthritis. In review of outcomes between the nurses and the general OPD, the following were measured and found:

	Doctor's Clinic		**Nurses' Clinic**
Deaths	3/118		1/86
Disability	Employment ↓	(p<0.05)	Employment ↑
Discomfort	No change	(p<0.05)	Reduction
Dissatisfaction	More	(p<0.01)	Less
Broken Appointments	X%	(p<0.05)	½X%
Use of Other Sources of Care	More	(p<0.05)	Less

Processes of supportive care for the five chronic conditions produced better outcomes than processes of technical care alone.

Hoekelman, R. A. "What Constitutes Adequate Well-Baby Care?" *Pediatrics* 55(1975): 3.

Two hundred forty-six healthy newborns were randomly allocated to four groups for Well-Baby care; six visits to an M.D., three visits to an M.D., six visits to a Pediatric Nurse practitioner, or three to a PNP.

No differences in any measure of care were found in knowledge, satisfaction, compliance, and health between the groups.

PRENATAL CARE AND FAMILY PLANNING

Smith, P. B.; Wait, R. B.; Mumford, D. M.; Nenney, S. W.; and Hollins, B.T. "The Medical Impact of an Antepartum Program for Pregnant Adolescents: A Statistical Analysis." *American Journal of Public Health* 68(1978): 169–172.

Adolescent pregnancy has rapidly become a major health and social problem. One hundred twenty-six pregnant adolescents were enrolled in a comprehensive antepartum program stressing prenatal care, and information on nutrition, labor, psychosocial aspects of pregnancy and contraception. Each class was a group encounter lasting three hours weekly. Median number of classes attended was seven. These adolescents were compared to a matched control group and the following significant differences resulted:

		Antepartum Program	Control
1.	Number of prenatal visits	6.3	5.1
2.	Admissions for false labor/person	.01	.41
3.	Caesarian delivery	4%	14%
4.	Birth weight (grams)	3,105	2,941
5.	Apgar score (mother <16 yrs)	9.0	7.6
6.	Urinary tract infection	1%	8%
7.	Post-partum return rate	74%	53%

Tietze, C. "What Price Fertility Control? Lower than that of Un-wanted Pregnancy." *Contemporary OB/GYN* 12(1978): 32–37.

The risks of birth control have been publicized lately, espe-cially when oral contraceptives (OCs), intrauterine devices (IUDs) or abortions are used. From all the available data in the United States and Britain, the author shows that the risk of mortality from childbirth is greater than the risk from birth control, but with im-portant exceptions:

DEATHS, PER 100,000 WOMEN (U.K. & U.S.)

Method	Age In Years					
	15–19	20–24	25–29	30–34	35–39	40–44
None (birth-related)	6	6	7	14	21	23
Abortion	1	2	2	2	2	1
OCs						
smokers	1	1	1	10	13	58
non-smokers	1	1	1	2	4	7
IUDs	1	1	1	1	1	1

The mortality related to having children is greater than that related to birth control except in older women who smoke and are on OCs.

Comment: The study deals with mortality only. IUDs and OCs are known to cause illness as well. Against this, however, must be considered the long-range morbidity of giving birth to unwanted children. Any morbidity or mortality in women due to contracep-tion is unfortunate; therefore effective contraceptive methods for men are needed.

THE ART OF CARING

Wright, W. B. "How to Examine an Old Person." *Lancet* 1(1977): 1145–1146.

Geriatrics is Medicine

How to Examine an Old Person

My elders tell me that there was a time when it was thought that "any doctor should be able to deal with any sick child." It is hard to imagine this statement being made nowadays and easy to see the reasons for the change in outlook. It is not so easy to understand yet that any special skill is required in the examination of an old person. For one thing, an old person is an adult like anybody else, and for another, the stakes are not so high. Yet elderly people represent one of the heaviest demands on the Health Service. The stakes of life and death do not weigh so heavily, certainly; what matters is to reduce invalidism or its effects sufficiently to make for a tolerable life in the community, rather than custodial care in a long-stay ward. The proper examination of an elderly patient is far more difficult than it seems at first sight. May I outline some general points which I have found helpful?

In taking the history it is of prime importance to establish clearly why the patient, or her relatives, have called you in at this time and not, say, a month or a year ago. Elderly illness is usually a composite of chronic conditions which have been present for some time, and acute incidents. It is the acute incidents which usually tip the scales so that the doctor is sent for. As often as not, something remediable, or at least supportive, can be done for the acute condition. Indeed, if the family make great play of chronic disabilities on calling you, the acute condition is probably minor.

Any sense of hurry will chase the most recent events out of the old person's head. You should consciously relax and allow her to speak freely, at least at first, without too much direct questioning. A chance remark often gives you an important clue. Always ensure that her mind has not slipped back to her previous illness. These patients are liable to talk in the same breath of symptoms experienced last week and last year.

You are not wasting a minute, sitting passively by your patient while she talks, if you use your eyes. A neglected house and garden means loss of energy or initiative. Poor hygiene means poor nutrition more often than not. The duration of incontinence may be evident from the smell of the house. If the house has no smell, family complaints of incontinence may be exaggerated. People tend to bias everything they say in the direction of the action they want you to take.

If possible, you should hold your patient's hand. Holding her hand reassures her, and there is much to be learned from a deliberate examination of the skin, fingers, joints and nails. At the same time feel her pulse. Gently feel for cogwheel rigidity in the wrist.

While she is talking at random about her complaints and symptoms, you should be studying her hair, face, eyes, and looking for involuntary movements. Has she a normal play of facial expression and good coordinated movements of both hands? Her neck veins may be visible. There may be a thyroid lump. She may be showing upper lid retraction at times. If the patient is lying under layers of clothing and bedding, think of myxœdema. Is her respiratory rate raised? This is a far more sensitive index of acute illness in the elderly than the temperature. Is the hemiplegic continually looking to one side? If so, it is highly likely that she is blind on the other side. This is extremely important in relation to which part of the bedroom her bed should be placed, for you may find that the only side on which she has sight is facing a blank wall.

Always begin your examination of the body at the back and let the patient cuddle a pillow. Old patients are not used to being examined, and they can tolerate examination of the back more readily. From the back you can examine the condition of the scalp, hair, the ears for tophi, the neck for glands, and the spine for scoliosis and tenderness on percussion. Spring the ribs for rib tenderness. Look for sacral œdema. The lower lobes are much more often affected than any other part of the lung, and they are accessible only from the back. Buttock rash can be due to thrush, and you may see the more characteristic buttock lesions from the back.

Having lifted up the nightie to the shoulders to examine the back first, you may now rest the patient back on the pillows, sitting upright, and you will find that the front of the garment comes up easily, so that you can now examine the anterior chest, with plenty of nightie above so that she will not be embarrassed. Do not forget to look at the neck, however; the trachea may be displaced or you may feel a firm retro-clavicular lymph-node which may tell you that she has carcinoma of the stomach. Gentle pressure on each carotid sinus in turn may give you an immediate explanation of recent syncopal attacks.

An apparent left ventricular heave is almost normal in the elderly, as are soft systolic murmurs, though elderly patients with systolic murmurs are more likely to have cardiac disease of some kind. In recent myocardial infarction the heart-sounds may be so soft as to be hard to hear. They are often better heard in the epigastrium, especially in obese people. The self-reporting of carcinoma of the breast is extremely poor in the elderly. You must not forget to feel for it, and for axillary lymph-nodes. Watch out for isolated areas of rib tenderness, because they often mean simple fracture and may be found without warning when an old person gets pneumonia after a recent fall. They may also represent carcinomatous deposits from some primary site.

Your patient will now be much more amenable to having the abdomen examined. Do not attempt this with the patient in a semi-reclined position. You will find nothing. She should now lie down with her head on not more than two pillows. If you find that the patient cannot do this without distress, then she is probably in congestive cardiac failure. Respiratory illness does not cause quite as much discomfort when the patient is supine. If, on lying flat, the patient shows a crease across the abdomen, then she has kyphosis or collapsed vertebrae. Make sure you distinguish between distension and obesity, if the abdomen is prominent. Do this by consciously gauging the thickness of the abdominal wall. Distension will most often be due to faecal impaction and colonic stasis, whatever the history you have been given. Rectal examination is essential to confirm this. A distended lower abdomen may represent a swollen bladder. It is an uncanny experience to find, and percuss out, a tense distended bladder in a patient who has made no complaint, and every geriatric physician finds this commonly. An irregular hard liver will tell you the diagnosis and prognosis, because it is almost always due to carcinomatosis which will be widespread elsewhere. If you find a hard, vertically eliptical tumour between the epigastrium and the umbilicus, ask yourself whether it pulsates, because if so it is a mildly aneurysmal abdominal aorta which is so common as to be a normal variant. The murmur which you often hear over this seems to have no significance in relation to the kidneys, but its presence might explain abdominal symptoms on a basis of mesenteric ischæmia, especially if there is weight-loss. In general, no palpable abdominal mass should be diagnosed until the patient has had an enema daily for several days. In most cases the mass will disappear.

A simple test of weakness of the upper limbs is to ask the patient to clap hands. Say "show me how you can clap hands" and do it with her. Elderly patients seem to respond to this joint activity with amusement. In the presence of the slightest weakness on one side, the other arm will dominate the handclapping. Where there is loss of body image, the other arm will dramatically clap empty air.

Your patient will not relax to let you examine her legs unless she is reclining comfortably with the abdomen and perineum covered. It is degrading for any patient to be wholly naked during medical examination, and especially so for the elderly. A towel placed over the lower abdomen and between the thighs allows full leg movement and hip joint examination. The rest of the area is adequately seen during rectal examination. Feel for the femoral pulse when looking for groin glands and hernial areas. Unilateral leg swelling, warmth, and suffusion will often tell you that there is a treatable cause of your patient's recent debility. You will also be surprised how often you find that one leg is truly shorter than the other in patients who walk badly. The cause is usually osteoarthritic hip damage, but sometimes unilateral Paget's disease and occasionally an impacted fracture. Always do passive movements before you test leg power. Hip rigidity may be the cause of apparent weakness. Do not ask the patient to "relax." It only makes her tense-up. If she is resisting every movement you make, it sometimes pays to say "now let me do it." When as part of your tests of muscle power you examine straight-leg raising, slip the palm of your hand under the opposite heel. The thrust into this palm will tell you how hard she is trying.

Knee-jerks are normally brisk and ankle-jerks diminished. The plantar response is often unhelpful, but ankle clonus is easier to elicit than you would expect. It truly confirms the presence of spasticity even where there is little paralysis. The discovery of a pressure blister on one heel can indicate that a mild stroke has occurred, affecting that side, even if there is little paralysis to be found.

You have not examined your patient properly until you see whether she can sit up unsupported and (if not too ill) stand or walk. Inability to walk is one of the most common reasons for being called in to deal with old people. There are only four causes—weakness, stiffness, pain, and loss of balance. This simple analysis will almost always put you on the right track and thereby considerably increase your chances of effective action.

Royal Devon and Exeter
  Hospital (Heavitree),
Exeter EX1 2ED

W. B. Wright

Prevention and Screening

LIFE-STYLE AND RISK FACTORS

Stinnett, P., and Whyte, M. "Lifestyle, Health and Disease: A Comparison between Papua New Guinea and Australia." *Medical Journal of Australia* 1(1978): 1–5.

The health of people in rural subsistence communities in a developing country was contrasted to those in urbanized, industrialized cities of Australia.

Parameters		Papua New Guinea	Australia
1.	Social cohesion	High	Low
2.	Infant mortality rate/1000	85	18
3.	Birth rate/1000	42	19
4.	Death rate/1000	15	9
5.	Five leading causes of death	pneumonia, diarrhea, dysentery, meningitis, malnutrition	heart disease, cancer, stroke, bronchitis, motor vehicle accidents
6.	Males per 100 females		
	6a. age 0 to 4	103	105
	6b. age 60 & over	188	66
7.	Diet per day (men)		
	7a. calories	2300	3165
	7b. protein %	3	13
	7c. fat %	2	35
	7d. carbohydrate %	95	52
8.	Weight change between ages 20 and 60	↓25%	↑25%
9.	Cholesterol (mg%)	148	250
10.	Diastolic pressure with age	↓	↑
11.	Smoking	rare	common

Papuan persons who live in the towns and thereby have contact with Western ways and diet begin to resemble European Australians in susceptibility to specific illnesses.

Comment: The results of this study lead us to speculate if *we* can have the best of both worlds—a bucolic environment free of major infections and malnutrition.

Tomasson, R. F. "The Mortality of Swedish and U.S. White Males: A Comparison of Experience, 1969–1971." *American Journal of Public Health* 66(1976): 968–974.

Life expectancy for American white men at birth is 67.9 compared to 71.9 for Swedes. From birth to 79, U.S. white male mortality exceeds Swedes' by 50 to 66%. The greatest differences are in ages under 1, 20–24, 50–59, representing infection, accident/homicide and cancer/cardiovascular-respiratory causes, respectively.

Social stress, family breakup, poorer safety standards, less physical activity, smoking, alcohol, and poor diet are all suggested differential factors.

Belloc, N. B., and Breslow, L. "The Relation of Physical Health Status and Health Practices." *Preventive Medicine* 1(1972): 409–421.

Seven thousand adults were followed for 5½ years. High life expectancy and good health were significantly related to the following habits:
1. three regular meals, no snacking;
2. daily breakfast;
3. moderate exercise 2 to 3 times a week;
4. seven to eight hours sleep at night;
5. no smoking;
6. no overweight; and
7. little or no alcohol.

A 45-year-old man with none or up to three of these habits has a remaining life expectancy of 22 years. One with six or seven of these habits has an expectancy of 33 more years. The health status of a middle-aged adult with all seven good habits is equivalent to a person 30 years younger with none.

Thomas, C. B. "Precursors of Premature Disease and Death: The Predictive Potential of Habits and Family Attitudes." *Annals of Internal Medicine* 85(1976): 653–658.

In a long-range "outcome" prospective study of medical students, definite links between original personality and suicide, mental illness, hypertension, and coronary occlusion were found relating to aspects of stress, lack of closeness to parents, anger, and methods of coping (including alcohol and cigarettes). Cause and effect are unknown but the interactions of stress and response on body defenses are supposed.

Marmot, M. G., and Syme, S. L. "Acculturation and Coronary Heart Disease in Japanese-Americans." *American Journal of Epidemiology* 104(1976): 225–247.

Coronary heart disease among Japanese men is lowest in Japan, intermediate in Hawaii, and highest in California, with differences not accounted for by diet, cholesterol, blood pressure, or smoking. The distinguishing factor seems to be traditional culture (lower rates) vs. Western acculturation (higher rates). This trend remains even when persisting traditionalists in the West and Western-acculturated in Japan are compared. Traditional cultures are more stable and have strong family-support systems.

Editorials, *Lancet:* 1) "Can I Avoid Heart Attack." 1(1974): 605–607. 2) "Prevention of Coronary Heart Disease." 2(1976): 738–784. 3) **Marmot, M., and Winkelstein, W., Jr.** "Epidemiologic Observations on Intervention Trials for Prevention of Coronary Heart Disease." *American Journal of Epidemiology* 101(1975): 177–181. 4) **Werko, L.** "Can We Prevent Heart Disease?" *Annals of Internal Medicine* 74(1971): 278–288.

These four articles, taken together, indicate that while multiple risk factors exist—such as smoking, hypertension, and increased blood lipids—they fail to predict the majority of heart attacks over any ten-year period. Mass intervention trials will therefore be highly inefficient, as reducing heart disease by attacking risk factors has a minimal effect. Even the known increased risk of heart attacks from hypertension and elevated cholesterol is not effectively reduced by treatment. While these assessments are gloomy, they do not reflect negatively on positive aspects, such as well-being and improved outlook, that weight control and no smoking produce. These decisions, however, are usually up to the individual to make.

McMichael, J. "Prevention of Coronary Heart-Disease." *Lancet* 1(1976): 1350–1351.

Eighty-three percent of those with *four* risk factors in the Framingham cardiovascular studies were alive after 10 years.

Rose, G.; Hamilton, P. J. S.; Keen, H.; Reid, D. D.; McCartney, P.; and Jarrett, R. J. "Myocardial Ischaemia, Risk Factors and Death from Coronary Heart-Disease." *Lancet* 1(1977): 105–109.

In a five-year follow-up of 18,403 British civil servants ages 40–64, 277 died of coronary heart disease (1.5%), half of whom had a suggestive history of angina/previous MI or abnormal ECG (ischemia).

The risk of dying of heart disease within the five-year period was most predictable by preexisting ischemia, and was worsened by other risk factors.

Risk of Dying (%)

		Ischemia	No Ischemia
1.	No ischemia	1%	
	Ischemia	5%	
2.	Ischemia at age:		
	40–49	1.5%	
	50–59	6.1%	
	60–64	6.8%	
3.		Ischemia	No Ischemia
	Smoking	4.7%	1.3%
	No smoking	4.0%	0.6%
4.	Systolic blood pressure (mm Hg)		
	<120	2.7%	0.7%
	120–139	4.3%	0.7%
	140–159	4.4%	0.9%
	>160	5.9%	1.9%
5.	Cholesterol (in mg %)		
	<180	3.3%	0.8%
	180–219	3.9%	0.9%
	220–259	4.1%	1.0%
	>260	8.4%	1.6%
6.	Blood sugar (2 Hr PP) (mg %)		
	<70	3.8%	1.0%
	70–89	4.3%	0.8%
	90–109	4.3%	1.1%
	>110	5.0%	2.4%
7.	Exercise		
	None	4.1%	1.4%
	Some	3.6%	0.9%
	Much	5.5%	0.9%

Even in the highest risk groups, the risk of dying is under 10% for five years. Screening and fitness intervention may be better directed to the better motivated group that already has ischemia—especially by lowering blood pressure, cholesterol, and weight, and use of moderate exercise.

Hammond, E.; Cuyler, B.; Garfinkel, L.; Seidman, H.; and Lew, E. A. "Tar and Nicotine Content of Cigarette Smoke in Relation to Death Rates." *Environmental Research* 12(1976): 263–274.

The first results are in. "Low tar–low nicotine" cigarettes provide some, but not much protection from heart disease and lung cancer.

STANDARDIZED DEATH RATES

	Heart Disease	Lung Cancer
Regular smokers	1.0	1.0
"Low-tar, low-nicotine" smokers	.84	.74
Non-smokers	.50	.11

THE INS AND OUTS OF SCREENING

Spitzer, W. O., and Brown, B. P. "Unanswered Questions About the Periodic Health Examination." *Annals of Internal Medicine* 83(1975): 257–263.

This article presents a comprehensive review of the "checkup." There are a number of conditions at different stages of life that are important to find, prevent, or treat:

Stage in Life	Targets for Selective Screening
The fetus and first year of life	Rhesus incompatibility with mother Phenylketonuria Congenital dislocation of the hip Some congenital heart defects
Preschool age	Hearing abnormalities Amblyopia Lead poisoning
Childhood and adolescence	Smoking Congenital heart defects
Adulthood	Smoking Breast cancer Cancer of the cervix Cancer of the colon and rectum Hypertension Bacteriuria in pregnancy
The aged	Hypertension Conditions and states amenable to rehabilitative intervention where the goal is not to cure or to extend life but to improve its quality.

Periodic health exams are being analyzed. Data from Kaiser-Permanente demonstrate a slight fall, not statistically significant, in the mortality of screened patients. Such studies are costly and require excellent patient compliance.

Checkups for asymptomatic people yielded 11% significant findings and 38% for symptomatic people. Fifty-nine percent of executives who died, died of undetected conditions in spite of periodic checkups. Much of this work can be done by extenders.

Lassek, W. "Value of Data Base Collection." Staff document. Rockville, Maryland: Division of Clinical Services, Bureau of Health Services, 1976.

In this "in-house" monograph, Lassek reviews the current information on screening for illness:

1.   While some studies do not show an increase in the detection of significant conditions in patients, some do. But in follow-up, compared to control groups, no consistent improvement in longevity occurred. Differences found in one disease (e.g., cancer), were either canceled by another (accidents) or were unrelated to the duration of follow-up. Where early detection occurs, it may serve only to expose the natural history at an earlier stage. Periodic screening picks up significant conditions in 2% of children (depending on which population is considered).

2.   Screening may cause psychosocial disease such as discrimination against persons with a sickle-cell trait and psychologic crippling of children erroneously diagnosed with cardiac disease.

3.   The more effective a screening test is in detection (sensitivity), the more false positives occur, resulting in rising costs for follow-up.

4.   The criteria for choosing which conditions should be screened are: a) the frequency of the condition; b) its effects on life; c) the ability to detect it in at an early stage; d) the degree to which the condition responds to early treatments; and e) the ability of providers to follow up abnormal results.

Delbanco, T. L., and Noble, J. "The Periodic Health Examination Revisited." *Annals of Internal Medicine* 83(1975): 271–273.

1.   Screening tests that are 95% sure of picking true positives (sensitivity) and 95% sure of excluding true negatives (specificity) generate many false positives which require further workup and cause anxiety. For a disease as prevalent as 2 per 100 random people, a positive test will be falsely positive 72% of the time.

2.   Routine testing in one study "found" presymptomatic disease in 1 to 5%; three-fourths of these tests became "normal" on retesting over a five-year followup.

Miller, R. E. "The Clean Colon." *Gastroenterology* 70(1976): 289–290.

Colon cancers grow slowly. One that is only 5 cm in diameter has taken at least four years to grow. A 1 cm cancer can be found on barium enema but requires a very clean colon—that is, fecal material must be well washed out. Twenty percent of cancers are missed on x-ray, mostly because of poor preparation. This figure indicates that 13,500 cases have been missed annually. "Clean colons" should be obtained 95% of the time. The five- and ten-year survival rate of localized cancers is 81%.

Altman, L. K. "Guidelines are Offered to Women on X-Rays to Find Breast Cancer." *The New York Times*, Tuesday, March 8, 1977, p. 16.

Mammography should be used:
a) when signs or symptoms of abnormal breast mass are present;
b) for women in a high-risk category who have a strong family history of cancer or have had previous breast cancer, and have not been pregnant before the age of 30; and
c) for periodic screenings of women over 50 years old.
In 106 women under 45 with breast cancer, 84% of the cases were found by the women themselves; 14% by their doctors in routine physical exams; and only 2% by mammography.
Radiation from mammography is potentially carcinogenic.

Weinstein, M. C., and Stason, W. B. *Hypertension: A Policy Perspective.* Cambridge, Mass.: Harvard University Press, 1976.

This book attempts to grapple with the cost-benefit issues in detecting and treating hypertension. Its conclusions:
1.   Treatment is costly.

2. Treatment is of uncertain efficacy in mildly hypertensive persons. This group consists of 70 to 80% of people with this condition.
3. Treatment can have side-effects from mild lassitude to impotence, to strokes in the elderly.
4. The costs to increase patient compliance are high.
5. The costs of detecting the very small proportion of people with immediately curable hypertension are high.
6. The improvement in outcome for those with initial diastolics over 90 on treatment is limited mostly to prevention of strokes at a reduction of 60 to 90% depending on age at start of therapy and duration of treatment.

Strategy	Cost ($)
1. Treat all Americans with diastolics over 105	900 million
2. Treat all Americans with diastolics over 95	2.9 billion
3. Treat all Americans with diastolics over 90	4.8 billion

Even with the first strategy, only 22% of the gross costs for treating complications of untreated hypertension are recoverable. Therefore, the "benefits" must be improvement of "life quality" and the costs must be regarded as a social expenditure.

---

1) **McNeil, B. J.; Varady, P. D.; Burrows, B. A.; and Adelstein, J. J.** "Cost-Effectiveness Calculations in the Diagnosis and Treatment of Hypertensive Renovascular Disease." *The New England Journal of Medicine* 293(1975): 216–221. 2) **McNeil, B. J., and Adelstein, S. J.** "The Value of Case-Finding in Hypertensive Renovascular Disease." *The New England Journal of Medicine* 293(1975): 221–226.

Nearly 25 million Americans are hypertensive—that is, their diastolic pressure is over 90 mm Hg. While medication offers control of blood pressure to most, 5 to 10% of hypertensives are potentially curable by surgery on diseased renal arteries (renovascular hypertension). Is there a strategy to detect this subgroup? How much would it cost, nationally? Is it worthwhile?

These three questions are explored with a mixture of analytic techniques once familiar only to systems analysts and economists. These techniques are: receiver-operating curves, sensitivity-specificity ratios, Bayes theorem, cost-effectiveness analyses, decision-analyses, and marginal costs.

The data analyzed by these techniques reveal the imperfectibility of medical care. Firstly, the two common screening tests for renovascular disease are the intravenous pyelogram and the iodohippuran renogram. Depending on how liberally the tests are interpreted, the more likely one or both tests in combination detect true renovascular disease, the more often they also detect disease that is not actually present. The converse is also true: if fewer misdiagnoses are made (when more stringent criteria are applied), then the number of detected cases will decrease. Whenever a screening test is positive, more elaborate diagnosis with arteriography may be undertaken.

Secondly, cure rates from surgery are only about 50% and those from operative mortality range from 3 to 10%.

Thirdly, while medication can control blood pressure in about 50 to 75% of completely compliant patients, usually 50% or less take medication faithfully, and side effects are common.

Fourthly, the cost of finding one potentially curable patient is about $2,000; the surgical cost of one cure is about $20,000. If all hypertensive Americans were screened, and those with renovascular disease treated, the total cost would be 10 to 13 billion dollars.

Fifthly, medical treatment is associated with better health outcomes for all types of hypertension if compliance is higher than 50% or diastolic readings are under 120. In any case, the differences in outcome between medical and surgical care never exceed 10%. This statistic indicates that only a handful of hypertensives should ever be subjected to screening tests in the first place.

By applying analytic techniques to medical care, several startling implications arise:

1.   Who is responsible for the health of a patient—the patient or the physician? Applying screening tests and possible surgery to those who don't comply with medicine sounds coercive.

2.   Once robust analyses of costs and benefits are available, who will decide for which interventions and diseases the public treasury can afford to pay? What other programs will then take lesser priority?

3.   Will analytic data be selectively interpreted in making what
are ultimately political decisions?

Korvin, C. C.; Pearce, R. H.; and Stanley, J. "Admissions Screening: Clinical Benefits." *Annals of Internal Medicine* 83(1975):
197–203.

Twenty different chemical and hematologic tests were rou-
tinely applied to 1,000 patients admitted sequentially to a general
hospital.

TESTS

19,980 test results in 1,000 patients

2,223 abnormal

1,325
no new diagnoses

675
predictable by clinical diagnosis

DIAGNOSES

223—leading to 83 new diagnoses in 77 patients

14
mild
diabetes

30
poor follow-
up, but might
have benefitted
from care

39
inconsequential

Conclusion: Routine screening may reveal many abnormal
tests but little good comes from this procedure. What little could
come from it is frittered away by physician inattention.

D'Souza, M. F.; Swan, A. V.; and Shannon, D. J. "A Long-Term
Controlled Trial of Screening for Hypertension in General Practice." *Lancet* 1(1976): 1228–1231.

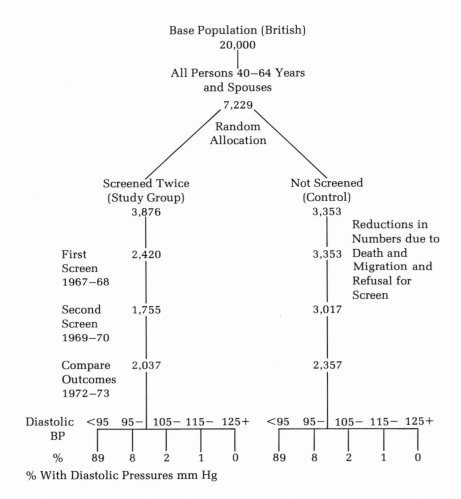

Base Population (British)
20,000

All Persons 40–64 Years
and Spouses
7,229

Random
Allocation

Screened Twice (Study Group) 3,876		Not Screened (Control) 3,353	
First Screen 1967–68	2,420	3,353	Reductions in Numbers due to Death and Migration and Refusal for Screen
Second Screen 1969–70	1,755	3,017	
Compare Outcomes 1972–73	2,037	2,357	

Diastolic BP	<95	95–	105–	115–	125+	<95	95–	105–	115–	125+
%	89	8	2	1	0	89	8	2	1	0

% With Diastolic Pressures mm Hg

Mass screening had no effect on outcome five years later, although it successfully identified new cases. One explanation is the tendency for BP to fall in 30% of untreated hypertensives.

"What Eyes and Ears Can Tell About the Heart." *Medical World News* 18 (January 10, 1977): 51.

The earlobe crease, when present, and corneal halo (arcus) are strong clues to the presence of coronary artery disease.

SCREENING OF CHILDREN

Londe, S.; Gollub, S.W.; and Goldring, D. "Blood Pressure in Black and in White Children." *Journal of Pediatrics* 90(1977): 93–95.

The incidence of elevated systolic pressures (over the 90th percentile for age and sex) in 710 black and 620 white boys, and in 585 black and 566 white girls, all ages 3–14 years, was 2.2% in the black children, 1.9% in the white children (not statistically different). From ages 3–14, mean systolic pressures rose from 96–97 to 110–119 and mean diastolic pressures rose from 59–62 to 66–67. No racial differences were found.

Random screening for hypertension in children produces little yield.

Metz, J. R.; Allen, C. M.; Barr, G.; and Shinefield, H. "A Pediatric Screening Examination for Psychosocial Problems." *Pediatrics* 58(1976): 595–606.

In San Francisco, screening for psychosocial problems, using automated, standardized forms, and paraprofessionals, shows about 7% new "positive" or "high risk" children. Half of this group seeks treatment whereas 4% of the no-risk group seek treatment. The variables associated significantly with high-risk were: race (black), less education in the mother, boys, and family turmoil.

Even though the screening technology is available, many barriers exist to intervention—parent motivation, provider caution, and lack of resources.

Bergman, A. B., and Stamm, S. J. "The Morbidity of Cardiac Non-Disease in School Children." *New England Journal of Medicine* 276(1967): 1008–1013.

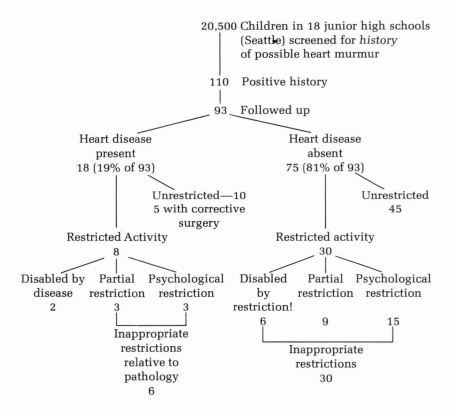

Therefore, in screening for heart disease:
  6/18   (33%) with heart disease and
30/75   (40%) without heart disease were inappropriately
                    restricted.
Considerably more harm than good was done by general screening for murmurs.

Maravilla, A. "The Early and Periodic Screening, Diagnosis and Treatment Program EPSDT. Lesson from a 10-Month Experience in North Texas." *Clinical Pediatrics* 16(1977): 173–178.

When 6,281 children from both rural and urban areas in Texas were examined in detail, 2,767 remediable medical problems were found:

Mental and physical abnormalities—694 (nearly all serious)

Laboratory abnormalities	—636 (anemia, blood or protein in the urine, sickle-cell disease, positive test for syphilis)
Abnormal hearing	— 51
Abnormal vision	—511
Positive TB tests	— 32
Incomplete immunizations	—843

Comment: Many of these children went untreated because the resources for follow-up, health education and remedies were not available.

PREVENTIVE STEPS THAT WORK (MOSTLY IN CHILDREN)

McDaniel, D. B.; Patton, E. W.; and Mather, J. A. "Immunization Activities of Private-Practice Physicians: A Record Audit." *Pediatrics* 56(1975): 504–507.

An audit of 13 private practice Idaho physicians with 813 two-year-old children showed the following results for complete immunizations:

	% Complete
Active patients (seen in last 12 months)	44%
Inactive patients	12%
Attended by private physicians only	38%
Attended by private physicians and public clinics	22%
Taken Alone	
DTP (3 doses)	76%
Polio (3 doses)	67%
Measles (1 dose)	62%
Rubella (1 dose)	60%

Marcuse, E. K. "Immunization: An Embarrassing Failure." *Pediatrics* 56(1975): 493–494.

Less than 40% of active patients of U.S. pediatricians had completed full immunizations by age two. Too often minor illnesses are falsely used as an excuse not to immunize. Every opportunity should be used to complete immunizations.

Editorial. "Towards the Prevention of Allergy." *Lancet* 1(1977): 339.

Children born to allergic parents (therefore genetically predisposed) show less eczema in their first year if kept off cow's milk for the first six months. Eczema in infancy is also a forerunner of asthma in childhood. Sensitization to environmental allergens seems to take place in the first six months, and cow's milk—perhaps through intestinal damage—encourages sensitization. Breast feeding is well known to decrease allergies, viral infections, and diarrhea.

Philipps, C., and Johnson, N. E. "The Impact of Quality of Diet and Other Factors on Birth Weight of Infants." *The American Journal of Clinical Nutrition* 30(1977): 215–255.

Low birth weight, especially for term babies ("small for dates"), is correlated with poorer development and ill health in infancy and early childhood. Nine maternal factors account for 86% of variability in birth weight as determined by multiple regression techniques.

Among them are:
1. weeks of gestation (positive if longer);
2. maternal diet (positive if good);
3. mother's age (positive if older);
4. mother's weight (positive if higher);
5. cigarettes smoked (negative); and
6. number of people in house (negative with more).

Gordis, L. "Effectiveness of Comprehensive-Care Programs in Preventing Rheumatic Fever." *The New England Journal of Medicine* 289(1973): 331–335.

Rates of rheumatic fever were lower in Baltimore census tracts with comprehensive programs than elsewhere. This decrease was largely achieved by reducing the complication following symptomatic sore throat through early treatment with penicillin.

Haverkorn, M. J.; Valkenburg, H. A.; and Goslings, W. R. O. "Streptococcal Pharyngitis in the General Population, I. A controlled Study of Streptococcal Pharyngitis and its Complications in the Netherlands." *The Journal of Infectious Diseases* 124(1971): 339–347.

Haverkorn, M. J.; Valkenburg, H. A.; Goslings, W. R. O.; Lorrier, J. C.; deMoor, C. E.; and Maxted, W. R. "Streptococcal Pharyngitis in the General Population, II. The Attack Rate of Rheumatic Fever and Acute Glomerulonephritis in Patients Not Treated with Penicillin." *The Journal of Infectious Diseases* 124(1971): 348–358.

Of 1,159 Dutch patients with a sore throat, 54% were positive for Group A Streptococci. Only penicillin eradicated the organisms, but did no better than aspirin in relieving symptoms.

Of 29 patients with rheumatic fever or glomerulonephritis only four had bad enough symptoms of sore throat to seek care. The risk of rheumatic fever and glomerulonephritis is lower in the general population than is the risk of sensitization to penicillin.

Weinstein, L., and Le Frock, J. "Does Antimicrobial Therapy of Streptococcal Pharyngitis or Pyoderma Alter the Risk of Glomerulonephritis?" *The Journal of Infectious Diseases* 124(1971): 229–231.

There is no proof that penicillin can prevent late glomerulonephritis.

The use of penicillin is justified because it decreases bacterial spread within the patient and the community.

Onion, D. K., and Taylor, C. "The Epidemiology of Recurrent Otitis Media." *American Journal of Public Health* 67(1977): 472–474.

Nearly one-half of 165 children with acute otitis media had at least one recurrent episode in the following year; 60% had a recurrence within four months. Hearing loss from an episode lasted over two weeks in 8%. The case for prophylactic antibiotics is a reasonable one at least after a recurrent bout.

Perrin, James M.; Charney, E.; MacWhinney, J. B.; McInerny, T. K.; Miller, R. L.; and Nazarian, L. F. "Sulfisoxazole as Chemoprophylaxis for Recurrent Otitis Media." *The New England Journal of Medicine* 291(1974): 664–667.

Twenty percent of children with otitis media have at least one recurrence. Recurrence increases risk of hearing loss. It has been found that 500 mg. of sulfisoxazole given twice daily, in a double-blind crossover study, reduced the recurrence rate by 57% in infants to five year olds—even in cases of incomplete compliance.

Bass, J. L.; Mehta, K. A.; and Truitt, L. "Safety Screening in a Pediatric Population." *The Journal of Pediatrics* 89(1976): 863–864.

Screening was done for accident-prevention in children by a three-question survey:
1. Are safety belts used?
2. Do parents know about preventing smothering?
3. Can children swim?
Nearly half the children surveyed were "at risk" for each question.

Access and Availability

BLOCKS TO ACCESS

Brook, R. H., and Williams, K. N. "Evaluating Quality of Health Care for the Disadvantaged: A Literature Review." Santa Monica, Calif.: The Rand Corporation, 1975.

There are several conclusions to this extensive review.
1. Health status is measurably worse in the poor.
2. The difference between the amount of care received by the poor and the amount received by the better off is not so great now, but the levels of use and appropriateness of care *in relation to need* are still lower for the poor.
3. The technical quality of care is generally the same for all classes, but considerable deficiencies also exist for all.
4. Attempts to improve quality by organizational approaches to health care delivery have had mixed results.

Frazier, P. J.; Jenny, J.; Bagramian, R. A.; Robinson, E.; and Proshek, J. M. "Provider Expectations and Consumer Perceptions of the Importance and Value of Dental Care." *American Journal of Public Health* 67(1977): 37–43.

Seventy-eight inner-city mothers who had need of dental care were interviewed, as were 316 dentists practicing in the city. The mothers believed education and dental care were more important than nice clothes, car or TV, while the dentists thought such inner-city women would rank the items in reverse order. Generally about half of the dentists thought inner-city people just didn't care about dental care; only 25% of the mothers held that view.

Access can be blunted by the subtle and not-so-subtle racial and class prejudices and attitudes of providers toward needy clients.

Lawson, I. R. "Health: A Demystification of Medical Technology." *Lancet* 1(1976): 481–482.

In Connecticut, the elderly have ready access to high-powered, high-priced hospital technology, but there are few facilities for rehabilitation and restoration outside the hospital. Day hospitals, rehabilitation units, home-makers and doctor house-calls are few and hardly consonant with need.

High-cost technology, with its control of education, insurance and prestige, curbs the development of medium and low-cost technology.

Hertz, P., and Stamps, P. L. "Appointment-Keeping Behavior Re-Evaluated." *American Journal of Public Health* 67(1977): 1033–1036.

It has been a common finding that poor or non-English-speaking health center clients break appointments ("no shows") up to 60% of the time. Usually the clients are blamed. But at a Model Cities Health Center (65% Medicaid, 69% Puerto Rican) the overall no-show rate was only 15%, with no difference between those on or off Medicaid. Puerto Ricans had nearly twice the no-show rate as English-speaking clients but only in those months when two Spanish-speaking staff members were absent, and when the clinic schedules changed rather confusedly. The organization clearly failed to communicate to non-English-speaking clients.

Stine, O. C.; Chuaqui, C.; Jimenez, C.; and Oppel, W. C. "Broken Appointments at a Comprehensive Clinic for Children." *Medical Care* 6(1968): 332–339.

Broken appointments were encountered more often in families with domestic strife and poor education.

Greenlick, M. R.; Freeborn, D. K.; Colombo, T. J.; Prussin, J. A.; and Saward, E. W. "Comparing the Use of Medical Care Services by a Medically Indigent and a General Membership Population in a Comprehensive Prepaid Group Practice Program." *Medical Care* 10(1972): 187–200.

When 1,500 poor urban families were brought into the Kaiser prepaid plan in Portland, Oregon, their rate of service use compared to the middle-class participants was essentially similar except that:
1.   poor adult males used more services for emotional problems; and
2.   poor people broke 25% of their appointments, compared to 8% of the other population.
"Many of the reported differences in the behavior of poverty populations appear to relate to differential access to care."

Alpert, J. "Broken Appointments." *Pediatrics* 34(1964): 127–132.

This is a review of 1,588 appointments at a university hospital pediatric OPD. Nineteen percent were broken but only 0.7% of those with a single, continuing physician were broken compared to 44% in the standard poor-person's clinic with no continuity of care.
Comparison of appointment keepers to non-keepers showed the following attributes:

	Keepers	Non-keepers
psychiatric problem	8%	27%
lowest social class	6%	25%
medical debts	37%	66%
found cost too high	4%	29%
previous visit cost > $11	13%	31%
no insurance	15%	26%
two or more sibs under two years	5%	18%

The data show that an overwhelming barrier to access is financial—either in direct costs for care or in indirect out-of-pocket costs (e.g., babysitting).

Hurtado, A. V.; Greenlick, M. R.; and Colombo, T. J. "Determinants of Medical Care Utilization: Failure to Keep Appointments." *Medical Care* 11(1973): 189–198.

Frequency of broken appointments increased proportionately with frequency of appointments. Frequent medical-care users and the indigent have higher rates (about 36%, compared to 16% for the better off). Broken appointments were unrelated to client criticisms of health plans. Cold weather and episodic care (as opposed to chronic care) were factors in the higher rates of broken appointments.

Comment: One way to reduce the number of broken appointments is to review the necessity for appointments, referrals, or follow-up visits.

Ambuel, P. J.; Cebulla, J.; Watt, N.; and Crowne, D. P. "Urgency as a Factor in Clinic Attendance." *American Journal of Diseases of Children* 8(1964): 394–398.

Broken appointments disrupt clinics: this paper surveys 2,939 appointments given to 174 patients at a university hospital pediatric OPD. The appointments were rated URGENT (must see within 48 hours), INTERMEDIATE (should be seen within one or two weeks), ROUTINE (could be seen a month later). Examples of the three are: pneumonia, strabismus, well-baby visit.

Type of appointment	N	% Broken
URGENT	(418)	10%
INTERMEDIATE	(1,723)	19%
ROUTINE	(798)	30%

The gradient existed for good appointment keepers (3 to 12%) as well as for poor appointment keepers (27 to 52%).

Comment: Are too many appointments being made? Could not several items of care (especially in prevention and screening) be accomplished in one visit—especially if physician extenders are used?

Bellin, S., and Geiger, H. J. "The Impact of a Neighborhood Health Center. Patients' Behavior and Attitudes Relating to Health Care: A Study of a Low Income Housing Project." *Medical Care* 10(1972): 224–239.

In a low-income housing project, use of the local (Tufts-affiliated) health center was extensive for both curative and preventive services. Services were free, and residents participated in center decisions.

CLIENT SURVEY

	Baseline Survey 1965	Follow-up 1967
Percent having "checkups"	17%	59%
Polio immunization in children	78%	92%
Delay in seeking care (percent of family members)	23%	10%
Satisfaction with care	24%	91%

Major elements contributing to satisfaction were access (60% of respondents), personal attention from staff (47%), quality of medical care (36%), and facilities (23%).

Long, K. Birth Control: Cheap, Available as Government Claims? *Seattle Post-Intelligencer*, 16 October 1977, p. C-3.

"When President Carter and HEW Secretary Califano ended federal funding of abortion last summer, they pointed to the widespread availability of cheap and effective birth control in this country. To check out their claims, the [Seattle] *Post-Intelligencer* asked a young woman reporter to pose as a young patient needing contraceptive information."

Source	Blocks to Access and Availability	Final Outcome
1. Private physician	Booked up for four months ahead	Prescribed the Pill over the telephone. No counseling.
2. Family Planning Foundation Clinic	Numerous forms, four-page survey on "quality of care," 2½ hour waiting time, extensive, unexplained physical exam and laboratory testing.	Got "a pack of Pills and an impression of rigorous professionalism." Little counseling.
3. Community Health Center	Cancelled appointment three hours before visit due to over-booking.	Referred to women's clinic.
4. Women's Clinic	Several bouts with barely audible tape-recorded phone answering service.	Relaxed, extensive counseling; discussed contraceptive alternatives to the Pill. Got one month's initial supply of pills.
5. University hospital clinic	Only benefits enrolled students; only 20% of U.S. colleges extend birth control services.	Thorough exam and excellent counseling.

Blocks to access to care, besides delayed appointments, excessive waiting, and others frequently cited, must also include excessively professional standards of care.

To overcome these blocks and others "took a lot more patience and persistence than I might have cared to dedicate if I hadn't been on assignment."

Unwanted pregnancies are most frequent among unwed teen-agers. "Had any of these [blocks to access] happened when I was a teen a few years ago, I doubt I would have persevered."

ACCESS AND THE ORGANIZATION OF CARE

Alpert, J. J.; Robertson, L. S.; Kosa, J.; Heagarty, M. C.; and Haggerty, R. J. "Delivery of Health Care for Children: Report of an Experiment." *Pediatrics* 57(1976): 917–930.

This study compares pediatric group practice (team-care, continuing primary care, preventive care, family care) to episodic care given to inner-city children (40% black, no Spanish).

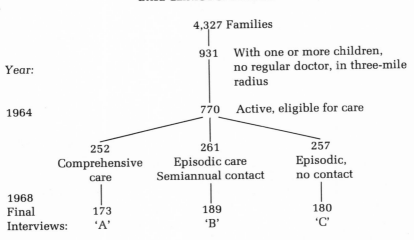

BASE CLINIC POPULATION

4,327 Families

931   With one or more children, no regular doctor, in three-mile radius

Year:

1964   770   Active, eligible for care

252   261   257
Comprehensive   Episodic care   Episodic,
care   Semiannual contact   no contact

1968
Final   173   189   180
Interviews: 'A'   'B'   'C'

B and C control did not differ and data presented on A and B groups only.

1. Preventive measures (% having)

	A	B
Fluoride	30	11
TB Test	70	47
Immunization Start	88	59
Immunization Finish	97	94
Polio Immunization	91	88
Measles Immunization	71	57
Tetanus Booster	92	81
Smallpox	55	44

    TB testing, fluoride outstandingly better in comprehensive care, immunization slightly so. Some in experimental group were "over-immunized."

2. Hospitalization rates per 100 children as the study progressed; 'A' had lower rates by about half (1.8 vs. 3.6 midway in the study) but became equal at the end (3.4 vs. 3.5).

3. Visits to doctor per 100 children

	Health Maintenance	Illness	Total
A	8.3	14.9	23.2
B	4.3	19.3	23.6

    Although total visits were equal, the distribution differed. The differences in illness visits were greater between A and B for families *not* on welfare.

4. Broken appointments

A	B
19%	38%

    In A the rate matched B as the study ended.

5. Satisfaction

    Brief waiting time was what satisfied group A mothers 1.6x as much as B. Difficulty in communicating with doctor was a complaint 9% in B, 2% in A. Actual contact time was 19 and 15 minutes for A and B, respectively.

6. Costs for lab tests and drugs

    Costs for A were roughly 50% of costs for B, mostly because of less frequent use of the laboratory (frequency of cultures, x-rays especially) due to "safety" factor in episodic clinic.

    Total costs were not computed; overhead of comprehensive care might have eaten up a considerable amount of the savings.

7.   Morbidity
    No differences in total health status were found.
    Conclusion: Continuing comprehensive primary care leads to
better satisfaction, less use of hospital and lab facilities and some
improvement in preventive care than does episodic care; overall
costs *may* be the same, and health status is not immediately affected. Welfare-status patients show even less differential than do
non-welfare patients, indicating that an ability to use the system is
also important.
    The argument for continuing, comprehensive care over avail-
able, accessible and competent episodic care is still not persuasive.

Gordis, L., and Markowitz, M. "Evaluation of the Effectiveness
of Comprehensive and Continuous Pediatric Care." *Pediatrics*
48(1971): 766–776.

    Two hundred twenty infants of first-time adolescent mothers
were randomly allocated to comprehensive care from a team (pedi-
atrician, public-health nurse and social worker) or to traditional
care (emergency room, well-baby and OPD clinics). One year later
no differences were found between the two groups in completeness
of immunization, use of care, morbidity or mortality. Furthermore,
no differences in compliance were found on a chronic regimen of
penicillin (for history of rheumatic fever).

Lee, M. W., and Adebonojo, F. O. "Tuberculosis among Urban
Black Children." *Clinical Pediatrics* 15(1976): 1055–1059.

    Tuberculosis rates for new cases and new skin-test conver-
sions were 177 and 673/100,000, respectively, in 2,700 children
(age two weeks to 19 years) in an urban ghetto. Children participating in a continuous, comprehensive health care program had the
same rates as those not participating.

Since adults are the principal repository of TB, case finding by adult health services is necessary.

Gold, E. M.; Stone, M. L.; and Rich, H. "Total Maternal and Infant Care: An Evaluation." *American Journal of Public Health* 59(1969): 1851–1856.

Comprehensive, continuing prenatal care to high-risk patients (those with a history of wastage, teenagers, the malnourished, grand multiparas, those with previous cesareans, hypertension and toxemia, or cardiac disease) reduces perinatal mortality (41%) and prematurity (29%).

Garfield, S. R.; Collen, M. F.; Feldman, R.; Soghikian, K.; Richart, R. H.; and Duncan, J. H. "Evaluation of An Ambulatory Medical-Care Delivery System." *The New England Journal of Medicine* 294(1976): 426–431.

Kaiser-Permanente designed a triage and health care system heavily staffed by paramedical workers that separated the well and the worried well (68.4%) from the sick (27.7%) and the asymptomatic sick (3.9%). Then they matched service to need:
1. Promotive-preventive care was provided for the well.
2. Preventive-maintenance care was available for the non-acutely ill.
3. Sick care was given to the acutely ill.
New patients had a 20-fold increase in access to physicians, and appointment waiting time fell from six–eight weeks to one or two days; the system reduced entry workup costs by 70-80%, and reduced total resources used by $32,550/1,000 entrants.

Comments: The high percentage of well patients undoubtedly promotes the savings to the system (most other practices report well patients at a 25% level of the practice) although large proportionate savings for sick care are also realized. Most of the savings are at the level of initial physician workup and routine return visits. Nothing is said about the reduction of "caring" time.

Mehl, L. E.; Bruce, C.; and Renner, J. H. "Importance of Obstetrics in a Comprehensive Family Practice." *Journal of Family Practice* 3(1976): 385–389.

Four family practices, two with obstetric services and two without, were examined:

Visit	With	Without
Total visits	3,058	2,199
Pregnancy	612	11
Total pediatric	716	71
Gynecology	500	187
Geriatric	225	524
Adult medical & acute	682	1,341
Orthopedic	122	6
Dermatology	37	26
Minor surgery	85	5
Psychotherapy	64	20

Inclusion of obstetrics broadens the *family* base of medical practice.

Yarnall, S. R. "Problems of Availability." In *The Changing Health Care Team: Improving Effectiveness in Patient Care*, edited by S. Zoog and S. Yarnall. Seattle, Washington: Medical Communications and Services Association (1976).

The author discusses a number of innovative strategies in health care delivery that deal with questions of access:

1. triage and service patients by type of encounter (acute, well-care, chronic) using different health care team members, instead of the "physicians only" pathway;

2. promote self-reliance with self-care protocols, extensive use of telephone consultation;

3. provide incentives for improved health habits and use of preventive care (rebates, for example);

4. use pamphlets in waiting room for education; make active use of waiting time;

5. use tickler file for routine health maintenance;

6. do wave scheduling where several patients are brought in together at fixed intervals through the hour (which promotes full use of all staff and facilities rather than having a linear flow bunching up at one station or another); and

7. extend service hours by off-hour schedules with pay and time-credit incentives for staff.

Enterline, P. E.; Salter, V.; McDonald, A. D.; and McDonald, J. C. "The Distribution of Medical Services Before And After 'Free' Medical Care—the Quebec Experience." *The New England Journal of Medicine* 289(1973): 1174–1178.

Two household surveys were carried out in the Montreal metropolitan area: one before the introduction of compulsory, universal health insurance (Medicare); and another a year and a half after its introduction. Information obtained included demographic characteristics; information on illnesses, selected symptoms and physician visits; attitudes toward services received; and information on convenience in obtaining services.

Results showed the following: physician visits per person per year increased among lower socio-economic groups; the proportion of symptoms for which a physician was seen increased from 62% before Medicare to 73% after Medicare; Medicare apparently increased waiting time for an appointment and in the doctor's office but had no effect on time spent to get from home to the doctor's office; the quality of care was considered worse after Medicare by all income groups, although lower income groups sought care more frequently under Medicare. Thus, economic barriers, which existed before Medicare, were removed, resulting in increased use by lower income groups and a shift in services from higher to lower income groups.

Patient Acceptability and Compliance

PATIENT SATISFACTION

Lebow, J. L. "Consumer Assessments of the Quality of Medical Care." *Medical Care* 12(1974): 328–337.

A review of consumers' perceptions of care: most studies indicate that consumers rate care highly, generally on the order of 70% positive, sometimes not in relation to "objective" measures of technical competence.

Comment: Retrospective satisfaction surveys seldom now reveal any new, useful information.

Hulka, B. S.; Zyzanski, S. J.; Cassell, J. C.; and Thompson, S. J. "Satisfaction with Medical Care in a Low Income Population." *Journal of Chronic Diseases* 24(1971): 661–673.

In a survey of low-income residents in Raleigh, North Carolina, satisfaction with care was related more to the provider's personal qualities (65%) than to professional competence (59%) or cost/convenience (49%).

Sussman, M. B.; Caplan, E. K.; Haug, M. R.; and Stern, M. R. "Chronic Patients in the Old Style Clinic" (Chapter 5) and "Chronic and Acute Patients in the Clinic" (Chapter 6). In *The Walking Patient: A Study in Outpatient Care.* Cleveland, Ohio: The Press of Western Reserve University, 1967.

A study from the old days of the Big Hospital Walk-in Clinic. Patient's satisfaction related to: 1) perception of the doctor as skilled; 2) the amount of time spent with the doctor; 3) presence of technical equipment; and 4) short waiting time. Chronically ill patients—more dependent, older, wedded to the system—were more often satisfied than acutely ill patients, who demand more of the system in speed of service and resolution of illness.

Korsch, B. M.; Gozzi, E. K.; and Francis, V. "Gaps in Doctor-Patient Communication 1. Doctor-Patient Interaction and Patient Satisfaction." *Pediatrics* 42(1968): 855–871.

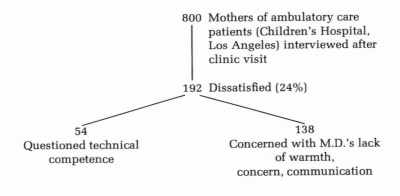

800 Mothers of ambulatory care patients (Children's Hospital, Los Angeles) interviewed after clinic visit

192 Dissatisfied (24%)

54 Questioned technical competence

138 Concerned with M.D.'s lack of warmth, concern, communication

---

Hines, B. L.; Clarkson, Q. D.; and Smith, D. D. "Development and Use of a Patient Satisfaction Questionnaire." *Journal of Family Practice* 4(1977): 148–149.

A survey in a university hospital family practice clinic showed clients' satisfaction was most closely correlated with perceived reassurance and information from the doctor and nurses. Access and waiting time were not correlated with overall satisfaction.

Cooke, C. L. "Patient Complaints against Physicians in the Richmond Area during 1973." *JAMA* 236(1976): 2643–2644.

Thirty-five formal complaints against physicians were registered with the Richmond (Virginia) Academy of Medicine in 1973. These broke down as follows (total exceeds 100%):

40%—excessive fee
35%—lack of availability
31%—therapy produced no cure
17%—faulty billing
11%—inaccurate diagnosis
11%—inadequate referral

PATIENT COMPLIANCE

Bergman, A. B., and Werner, R. J. "Failure of Children to Receive Penicillin by Mouth." *The New England Journal of Medicine* 268 (1963): 1334–1338.

This classic study, now 15 years old, undermines many favorite theories that relate patient knowledge to compliance. At the Syracuse Memorial Hospital 70 children from blue-collar families were given a ten day course of oral penicillin. Fifty-nine were followed up, and parents were questioned, to determine the following:

Adequate knowledge of diagnosis	—80%
Adequate knowledge of drug and dosage	—93%
Difficulty giving drug	—22%
Claimed *all* doses given	—83%

By pill count or liquid measure:

Drug actually stopped by day 3	—56%
Drug actually stopped by day 5	—71%
Drug actually stopped by day 9	—82%

Nine assays for penicillin in 41/59 children confirmed the findings.

Sackett, D. L., and Haynes, R. B., eds. *Compliance with Thera-peutic Regimens.* Baltimore: Johns Hopkins University Press, 1976.

Already a classic in its field:
Chapter 1:

Four possibilities exist.

		Outcome	
		Good	Poor
Compliance	Good	Desired	Therapy inadequate
	Poor	Incorrect diagnosis Unnecessary treatment	System failed

Poor outcome with poor compliance suggests some remediable defect in care or communication.

The ethics of "improving" compliance are also discussed.
Chapter 2: *The magnitude of the problem*
A review of 40 studies shows in general that:
1. symptomatic patients keep 80% of their appointments; asymptomatic patients keep 50% of their appointments;
2. compliance with short-term medication decreases rapidly by the day; and
3. 50% of patients on long-term therapy are compliant.
Often, however, far less treatment than prescribed is needed.

Chapters 3–4: *"Proved" factors correlating with non-com-pliance*

1.	Diseases	Psychiatric diagnosis
2.	Regimen	Complex schedule, long duration, high cost, requiring behavior change, and several drugs at once
3.	Source of therapy	Inconvenient or inefficient clinics
4.	Patient-provider interaction	Patient dissatisfaction, poor supervision, little feedback to patient

5.　Patient　　　　Inappropriate health beliefs, previous non-compliance, family instability, extreme youth or age

Chapter 5: *Methods of measuring compliance*

Blood levels, urine excretion, outcome, interview, pill count, prescription filling, side-effects.

Chapter 6: *How to improve compliance*

Various strategies have been tried:

EDUCATIONAL

Fixed-content health messages

Flexible counseling

Counseling plus written instructions

Programmed instruction

Lectures

Role-playing

BEHAVIORAL

Simpler dosage schedules

Behavior modification

Telephone reminders

Blood drug monitoring plus supervision

Home visits

Free drugs

Continuous care

Convenience

Educational methods increased compliance on an average of 64%, and behavioral methods by 85%.

Chapter 7: *Patient education*

Little evidence that traditional patient-education approaches make any difference in compliance.

Chapter 8: Involving the patient (and parents, in the case of children) in his/her own therapy increases compliance.

Chapter 9: *Behavior modification*

Identify the environmental events that trigger compliance or non-compliance, and reward (praise, usually) or emphasize the former, criticize or change the latter. Use all members of health care team. Try to set a patient-contract: individualized, written, owned by the patient.

Chapters 10–11: Tailoring of regimens to patient's convenience.

Chapter 12: Use of pharmacists as educators or as givers of information increases compliance slightly.

Chapters 13–15: Research priorities and methods.

Blackwell, B. "Patient Compliance." *The New England Journal of Medicine* 289(1973): 249–252.

Of drugs prescribed, 50% are not "taken as directed."

Non-compliance was associated with patients who were chronically ill, very young or very old, women under 30, poor and under-educated; with poor doctor-patient relationships; with complex regimens; and with a lack of information.

Francis, V.; Korsch, B. M.; and Morris, M. J. "Gaps in Doctor-Patient Communication: Patients' Response to Medical Advice." *The New England Journal of Medicine* 280(1969): 535–540.

Of 800 Los Angeles parents of pediatric clinic visitors: 38% were moderately compliant; and 11% were non-compliant.

Correlating with non-compliance were lack of warmth in doctor-patient relations, lack of explanations, complexity of treatment, and lack of satisfaction.

Severity of illness *increased* compliance.

Brand, F. N.; Smith, R. T.; and Brand, P. A. "Effect of Economic Barriers to Medical Care on Patients' Noncompliance." *Public Health Reports* 92(1977): 72–78.

In 290 general-hospital patients discharged with prescriptions, non-compliance was related to less education, lower income, severer disease, multiple prescriptions, number of times a prescription was taken per day, and high cost of prescriptions.

McKenney, J. M.; Slining, J. M.; Henderson, H. R.; Devins, D.; and Barr, M. "The Effect of Clinical Pharmacy Services on Patients with Essential Hypertension." *Circulation* 48(1973): 1104–1111.

A pharmacist spent about the same time with a patient as did the physician (30 minutes of initial contact, 6 minutes for subsequent contacts) providing information about hypertension and the drugs, and information on other mild, self-limited conditions.

Comparing 25 study patients and 25 control patients, a marked increase in knowledge, compliance and normal blood pressure was seen in the group getting the extra attention. Access to information from a caring provider seems most important to compliance.

Finnerty, F. A.; Mattie, E. C.; and Finnerty, F. A., III. "Hypertension in the Inner City. I. Analysis of Clinic Dropouts." *Circulation* 47(1973): 73–75.

Sixty dropouts were interviewed to find the reason for noncompliance. Excessive waiting time (2.5 hours for doctor, 1.8 hours for pharmacy) and poor doctor-patient relations, with no continuity, were causes. Reorganization of clinic, based on the client survey, decreased the drop-out rate from 42% to 8%.

Fletcher, S. W.; Appel, F. A.; and Bourgois, M. "Improving Emergency-Room Patient Follow-Up in a Metropolitan Teaching Hospital." *The New England Journal of Medicine* 291(1974): 385–388.

Addition to an emergency room of a follow-up clerk who provided appointment reminders and acted as guide and ombudsman through clinic procedures increased the return rate from 58% (control group) to 80% (intervention). Improved compliance was unrelated to demographic characteristics of the patients.

Finnerty, F. A.; Shaw, L. W.; and Himmelsbach, C. K. "Hypertension in the Inner City. II. Detection and Follow-Up." *Circulation* 47(1973): 76–78.

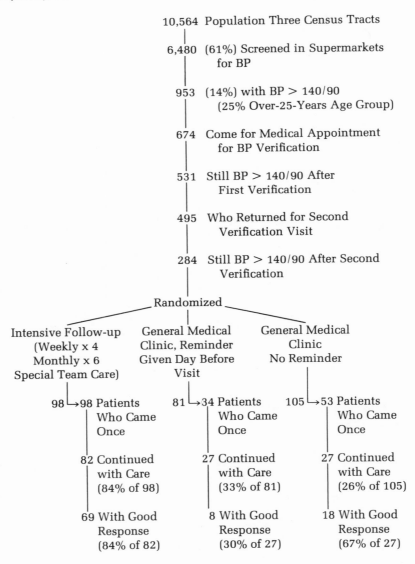

10,564 Population Three Census Tracts

6,480 (61%) Screened in Supermarkets
for BP

953 (14%) with BP > 140/90
(25% Over-25-Years Age Group)

674 Come for Medical Appointment
for BP Verification

531 Still BP > 140/90 After
First Verification

495 Who Returned for Second
Verification Visit

284 Still BP > 140/90 After Second
Verification

Randomized

| Intensive Follow-up (Weekly x 4 Monthly x 6 Special Team Care) | General Medical Clinic, Reminder Given Day Before Visit | General Medical Clinic No Reminder |

98 →98 Patients
Who Came
Once

81 →34 Patients
Who Came
Once

105 →53 Patients
Who Came
Once

82 Continued
with Care
(84% of 98)

27 Continued
with Care
(33% of 81)

27 Continued
with Care
(26% of 105)

69 With Good
Response
(84% of 82)

8 With Good
Response
(30% of 27)

18 With Good
Response
(67% of 27)

Compliance, as measured by returning for follow-up verifications, could be increased from 50% to 100% by personal contact.

Compliance, as measured by staying with treatment, could be increased from 26–33% to 84% by continued contact with a special team, especially paramedical members. Continued contact gave improvement in BP outcome. Ten percent of those *initially* found with elevated BP had a "good" outcome (although follow-up of dropouts was not available for comparison), brought about by a labor-intensive program.

Inui, T. S.; Yourtee, E. L.; and Williamson, J. W. "Improved Outcomes in Hypertension After Physician Tutorials. A Controlled Trial." *Annals of Internal Medicine* 84(1976): 646–651.

Training physicians in cultural, psychological and perceptual causes of patients' non-compliance helped these doctors to spend more time addressing these issues and less time following the physiological data-base.

Blood pressure control was achieved for more patients of these physicians than for patients of control (untutored) physicians, and the patients' knowledge of and compliance in pill-taking (but not appointment keeping) were significantly enhanced.

"Patient Compliance-Motivation by Contract." *Medical World News* 17(1976): 9.

Nurse practitioners at the University of Michigan regard patients as "consumers who buy our health services"; therefore, they provide incentives for compliance with payoffs like lottery tickets, pornographic magazines, and brief waiting times in the office.

Groves, J. E. "Taking care of the hateful patient." *New England Journal of Medicine* 298(1978): 883–887.

Even while we seek to make care "acceptable" and to get patients to participate in, or at least comply with their care, we must recognize that a certain proportion cannot or will not for deep-seated psychological reasons.

Patient Type	How They Present	Reaction Evoked in Provider	Suggested Management
1. The dependent CLINGER	Repeated and seductive requests for attention, explanations, remedies; bottomless need and emotional (child-like) dependency & gratitude.	Power and specialness leading to weary aversion	Set limits early; avoid making promises that cannot be kept or feeding illusions of omnipotence that will shatter.
2. The entitled DEMANDER	Hostile, intimidating, deservedness (a defense against abandonment or knowledge of dependency).	Depression, fear and rage	Never deny the entitlement (the only defense the patient has) but re-channel it toward indicated regimen ("You are entitled to this good care, but we need your help, etc.").
3. The manipulative HELP-REJECTOR	Pessimistic, nay-saying, believes nothing helps; one symptom replaces another; smugly reports that the treatment didn't work. The "crock" uses symptoms to stay "married" to the provider.	Anxiety, over-diagnosis, over-treatment	Share the pessimism, don't either get too close or reject; be firm and consistent. See regularly at provider-determined intervals.

Patient Type	How They Present	Reaction Evoked in Provider	Suggested Management
4. The major DENIER	Denial without self-destructive intent, prizing independence and chafing under any restriction (such patients actually survive longer than non-deniers). Tend to be likeable and hard-working.	Anxiety, impatience, chagrin	Work lightly and cheerfully with the denier. Avoid doomsday talk, appeal to sturdiness.
5. The self-destructive DENIER	Displays unconscious self-murderous behavior; furiously defeats attempts to save life—for example, alcoholics.	Malice; hateful wishes for patient to die; heroics or total resignation	Recognize limitations of patient and feelings evoked in provider.

Negative, disowned, or denied feelings in the doctor lead to errors in diagnosis and treatment.

Major Errors

ERRORS IN THE PRESCRIPTION AND USE OF DRUGS

Editorial. "Drugs and the Elderly." *Lancet* 2(1977): 693–694.

1. The elderly are 12% of the population, account for 33% of drug costs.
2. Differences in metabolism of the elderly (fat storage, liver metabolism and kidney excretion) delay the elimination and therefore increase the effects of drugs.
3. Multiple drugs are often prescribed to the elderly with resulting increase in adverse interactions, and errors in compliance.
4. Twelve percent of hospital admissions to geriatric units are due to drug reactions.
5. Sixty percent of elderly clinic patients make one or more medication errors, 25% of which are serious.

Hulka, B. S.; Cassell, J. C.; Kupper, L. L.; and Burdette, J. A. "Communication, Compliance, and Concordance between Physicians and Patients with Prescribed Medications." *American Journal of Public Health* 66(1976): 847–853.

This study of 46 physicians and their 35 private patients with diabetes or heart failure on medication noted four types of medication errors:

Omission (19%)
Commission (19%)
Scheduling misconception (17%)
Non-compliance (3%)
                58% error rate

Error rate increased with:
    multiplicity of drugs;
    complexity of schedules; and
    patient's unawareness of drug function.
No consistent pattern of patient characteristics or disease severity
was found to affect error rate.

Stevens, J. "Barbiturate Prescribing as an Indicator of Therapeutic
Process." *Lancet* 2(1976): 946–948.

A private practitioner believes he has improved his care of
patients by ceasing all prescriptions for hypnotics and developing
minor skills in counseling, taking five- to ten-minute sessions at
weekly intervals per patient. Regular prescription of hypnotics reveals the following about a practice:
1.   a negative approach to a *symptom*;
2.   a readiness to prescribe on demand;
3.   a readiness to prescribe repeated doses;
4.   an acceptance of life-long habituation;
5.   an uncritical use of new and potent drugs; and
6.   an uncritical assumption that loss of sleep is in itself bad,
    trading off loss of REM sleep for total hours not awake.

Galton, L. "Know Your Medications, Stop Taking Risks!" Parade
Magazine (*The Boston Globe*) 9 January 1977.

A review from a Sunday supplement on the failure of patients
to use drugs at the right times, in the right amounts or at all. The
common causes are:
1.   poor prescription writing and communication of instructions
    to patient;
2.   physicians' unawareness of some uses of drugs;
3.   physicians' unawareness of maximum effectiveness of drugs
    (time, dosage, ancillary techniques);

4.   patients' failure to take drugs at all (35–75% failure rates for common drugs); and
5.   patients' failure to ask about side effects.

Furstenberg, M. D.; Taback, M.; Goldberg, H.; and Davis, J. W. "Prescribing, An Index to Quality of Medical Care: A Study of the Baltimore City Medical Care Program." *American Journal of Public Health* 43(1953): 1299–1309.

This article is an early (1953) demonstration that a review of prescribing patterns could affect quality of care and costs by moving to generic drugs, fewer drugs and refills, and minimal duration of therapy.

Larkin, J. K., and Wertheimer, A. I. "Old Drugs at Home." *The New England Journal of Medicine* 298(1978): 857.

In 20 suburban households surveyed, the following was found:
1.   average drugs per household—12;
2.   average age of prescriptions—20 months (1–51, range);
3.   % drugs used within last month—42%;
4.   % households with drugs used by a person other than the initial user—41%;
5.   category of action:
       psychotropic   —23%
       respiratory   —31%
       dermatologic   —17%
       vitamins   — 7%
       antimicrobials — 7%
       digestive   — 7%
       cardiovascular— 1%
       miscellaneous — 8%; and
6.   the total number of drugs identified—239.

Kunin, C. M.; Tupasi, T.; and Craig, W. "Use of Antibiotics: A Brief Exposition of the Problem and Some Tentative Solutions."*Annals of Internal Medicine* 79(1973): 555–560.

More than 50% of the antibiotics used in hospital are not needed, are not appropriate, or are given in incorrect dosages. One or two expensive, new antibiotics often account for 70% of all antibiotic costs in hospital. Administrative controls are required.

Schimmel, E. M. "The Hazards of Hospitalization." *Annals of Internal Medicine* 60(1964): 100–110.

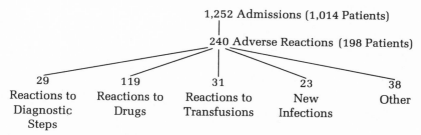

1,252 Admissions (1,014 Patients)

240 Adverse Reactions (198 Patients)

29	119	31	23	38
Reactions to Diagnostic Steps	Reactions to Drugs	Reactions to Transfusions	New Infections	Other

20% adverse reaction rate per hospitalization, the plurality for drugs.

Rabin, D. L.; Bush, P. J.; and Fuller, N. A. "Drug Prescription Rates before and after Enrollment of a Medicaid Population in an HMO." *Public Health Reports* 93(1978): 16–23.

One thousand poor people were enrolled in a pre-paid group-practice HMO. Service utilization and drug use after enrollment were studied and compared to those of a Medicaid control group.

		Enrollees	Control
1.	Encounters per person	3.5	3.9
2.	Drug costs per person	$15.51	$26.11
3.	Prescriptions per visit	.63	.68
4.	Generic drug prescriptions	10%	8%
5.	Irrational drug prescriptions	22%	18%

Costs were lowered largely by having fewer encounters and slightly fewer prescriptions per visit. The quality of drug prescriptions was *not* improved in the HMO.

"Adverse Interactions of Drugs." *The Medical Letter* 19(1977): 5–12.

"Two or more drugs administered at the same time or in close sequence may act independently, may interact to increase or diminish the intended effect of one or more of the drugs, or may interact to cause an unintended reaction."

This issue of *The Medical Letter* lists over 100 adverse effects of pairs of drugs that interact. More undoubtedly exist. There is yet little information on drug interactions with common food additives. The majority of potentially dangerous interactions exist with commonly used drugs or chemicals such as aspirin, alcohol, tranquilizers, antimicrobials, and drugs used to treat hypertension, diabetes, heart disease and clotting disorders. Some of the interactive drugs are those bought over-the-counter, such as aspirin, alcohol, and vitamin E.

The *Medical Letter* concludes: "As few drugs as possible should be prescribed for concurrent use."

OTHER COMMON ERRORS

"Latest Findings on All U.S. Claims." *Medical World News* 17 (1976): 34.

The pattern of malpractice suits in 1975–1976 shows claims against surgical procedures leading the list (80%), with minor surgery at the top (18%). Claims on nonsurgical cases were 15% of the total number of claims. Audits for major errors in ambulatory care, therefore, should clearly review minor surgery.

Jackson, G.; Pierscianowski, T. A.; Mahon, W.; and Condon, J. "Inappropriate Antihypertensive Therapy in the Elderly." *Lancet* 2(1976): 1317–1318.

Treatment of hypertension in the elderly, not symptomatic from the elevated pressure, is more apt to do harm than good by lowering blood pressure and thus by perfusion through arteriosclerotic arteries, leading to symptoms of hypotension or strokes.

Editorial. "Cardiogenic Dementia." *Lancet* 1(1977): 27–28.

Old people with dementia or senility are often written off and sent to nursing homes; many times senility is reversible, as suggested by this article. Congestive heart failure or slow heart rates can reduce blood flow to the brain.

Greitzer, L.; Stapleton, F. B.; Wright, L.; and Wedgwood, R. J. "Telephone Assessment of Illness by Practicing Pediatricians." *Journal of Pediatrics* 88(1976): 880–882.

Based on standards developed by the American Academy of Pediatrics for triage questions to be asked over the telephone on specific complaints, pediatricians asked only 52% of the possible questions (those more experienced asked even fewer). *Crucial* questions (about difficulty of breathing in cough; state of hydration in diarrhea; abdominal pain with vomiting; character of a rash) were asked less than 50% of the time.

Assurance

Nelson, A. R. "Orphan Data and the Unclosed Loop: A Dilemma in PSRO and Medical Audit." *The New England Journal of Medicine* 295(1976): 617–619.

Utah's PSRO experiences were reviewed:
1. Only 10–20% of physicians work at setting criteria.
2. Whenever compliance levels fall below 70%, physicians— especially those who refused to help set the criteria—attack the validity of the criteria.
3. Expert-developed criteria were developed for 120 diagnoses. Twenty-nine diagnoses were audited, representing 4,500 hospital cases and 100,000 criteria elements. Results (below) were greeted—even by local audit committees—with "So what?"

DX	Criterion	Pre-Audit	Compliance Post-Audit and Education
Diabetes	Examine eye ground	64%	62%
Intestinal bleeding	Prothrombin time	61%	62%
Phlebitis	Homan's sign	56%	44%
	Pelvic and rectal exam	43%	44%
	Chest x-ray	74%	75%

The only improvement in care was seen in increased use of packed red-cell transfusions for stable, non-hemorrhaging cases. This, because it was a *discrete, proved, high-impact* process, was taught face-to-face very close to the time of actual transfusion.

Hare, R. L., and Barnoon, R. L. *Medical Care Appraisal and Quality Assurance in the Office Practice of Internal Medicine.* Springfield, Va.: National Technical Information Service, PB–237 943, 1973.

Private internists set criteria for diagnosis and therapy of six medical conditions. The same physicians returned questionnaires detailing actual performance for patients with these conditions.

"There was little or no correlation between theoretical criteria and actual performance." Performance ratings (0–100), based on their own criteria, were 49–71% with a median of 61%.

Editorial. "Audit of Audit." *Lancet* 2(1976): 453.

Surgical and medical audit at Cornell Medical Center produced the following results:
1.   a review of 9,500 hospital records took place, and 6 patients who stayed too long were identified; audit cost: $34,212 per patient. No change in average length of stay; and
2.   fifteen medical audits had no effect on medical behavior; audit cost: $71,821.

Fries, J. F. "A Data Bank for the Clinician?" *The New England Journal of Medicine* 294(1976): 1400–1402.

To assist clinicians in providing the best therapy appropriate to condition and prognosis, this paper recommends a computer data bank which stores patient characteristics (illness, age, biochemical and physical findings) against outcome probabilities and best therapy. The cross tabulations are similar to what an experienced clinician goes through in management of a case. See table below.

INDIVIDUALIZED STUDIES IN SYSTEMIC LUPUS ERYTHEMATOSUS

Patient Characteristics	Outcome at 18 Mo. (%)			Best Therapy (Mg/Day)
	Death	Rash Increase	Proteinuria	
55-year-old man with hematocrit of 42.5%, complement of 85 & urine protein of 0	0	17	23	Aspirin (1500)
26-year-old woman with hematocrit of 38.9%, & complement of 115	3	27	37	Prednisone (12)
20-year-old woman with hematocrit of 35.5%, complement of 73 & urine protein of 2+	17	28	32	Prednisone (30)
24-year-old woman with creatinine of 1.1 mg/100 ml, urine protein of 3+ & hematocrit of 27%	30	39	40	Prednisone (30) & azathioprine (100)

Williamson, J. W.; Alexander, M.; and Miller, G. E. "Continuing Education and Patient Care Research." *JAMA* 201(1967): 118–122.

Physicians responded appropriately to only ⅓ of unexpected abnormal lab results, even after conferences and newsletter reminders. Physically masking abnormal data on the charts with removable tape doubled the response rate; but after six months the rate fell to 1.5 times the baseline.

McDonald, C. J. "Protocol-Based Computer Reminders, the Quality of Care and the Non-Perfectibility of Man." *The New England Journal of Medicine* 295(1976): 1351–1355.

On-line computer-based protocols took data from ambulatory encounters and, based on certain events, issued prospective reminders to physicians in three categories based on a "trigger event":

1. observe a physical finding or inquire about a symptom ("trigger event": angina—inquire about frequency if on nitroglycerin);
2. order a diagnostic study ("trigger event": measure BUN if patient is on reno-toxic drugs); and
3. change or initiate therapy ("trigger event": increase potassium supplements because last potassium was low and patient is on a diuretic).

In a controlled study, physicians acting as their own control *before* and *after* computer-reminder program responded to 51% of 327 trigger events when the computer reminded them and 22% of 385 trigger events without computer. The training effect disappeared in the second control period.

In retrospective review of computer suggestions, physicians agreed with the protocol logic 77% of the time.

Conclusion: failure of physicians to assure quality is due not to ignorance but to information overload (man's limitation as data processor), and *prospective* reminders are useful.

Jones, S. R.; Barks, J.; Bratton, T.; McRee, E.; Pannell, J.; Yanchick, V. A.; Browne, R.; and Smith, J. W. "The Effect of an Educational Program upon Hospital Antibiotic Use." *American Journal of the Medical Sciences* 273(1977): 79–85.

In a university hospital five categories of antibiotic use were defined:

1) appropriate;
2) ineffective;
3) expensive/toxic;

4)   improper dosage; and
5)   unjustified.

Before and after an intense educational program the following prevalences (% of total orders) of use were found:

Category	Before	After
1	6%	15%
2	7%	9%
3	13%	2%
4	9%	9%
5	33%	30%

Education only increased the use of less expensive, alternative drugs, and this was due mostly to discontinuing one drug (cephalexin). Institutional control, i.e., a regulated formulary, is the only proved and inexpensive means of control and assurance.

Lewis, C. E., and Hassanein, R. S. "Continuing Medical Education—An Epidemiologic Evaluation." *The New England Journal of Medicine* 282(1970): 254–259.

An epidemiologic survey of the effect of continuing medical education on medical outcomes (perinatal and maternal deaths and high rates for certain operations) in Kansas shows no correlation. Reasons may be that only a small number of physicians (7%) took 50% of the total hours available; or that many other factors determine outcomes; or that education must be explicitly linked to individual practice.

Buck, R. Jr., and White, K. L. "Peer Review: Impact of a System Based on Billing Claims." *The New England Journal of Medicine* 291(1971): 877–883.

In an attempt to enforce changes in provider behavior, one medical care foundation tied audits to the fee-for-service billing structure. Specific procedures which fell in frequency after the audits were intramuscular injections, hospital and initial office visits. The total number of office visits, however, increased.

Comment: The study illustrates the aphorism that: "You cannot do just one thing."

Methods of Assessment

Explicit Process Criteria

Falk, I. S.; Schonfeld, H. K.; Harris, B. R.; Landau, S. J.; and Milles, S. S. "The Development of Standards for the Audit and Planning of Medical Care: Concepts, Research Design and the Content of Primary Physician's Care." *American Journal of Public Health* 57(1967): 1118–1136.

This method develops a lengthy set of indices for evaluating the content of medical care. Fifty-seven physicians in private practice and with clinical faculty appointments at Yale were interviewed and their expert judgments were elicited on 230 disease categories that account for 90% of all the conditions that physicians deal with. The diseases are those commonly considered to require some professional or technical care.

The clinicians were asked to state what practices constitute optimum medical care for specific diseases. They stated preferences about the kinds and amount of required services, the types of consultations, and the lengths of treatment. Interviews were recorded and then developed into narrative accounts of what comprises good care in each of the disease groups or conditions. The interview data was analyzed and expressed quantitatively for each category.

The indices constructed from these expert judgments are valuable because they serve as tentative standards to describe good medical care. Furthermore, actual health care can be measured against them. The relationship of these criteria to what designers do in actual practice and to patient outcomes are unmeasured.

Goetzl, E. J.; Cohen, P.; Downing, E.; Erat, K.; and Jessiman, A. G. "Quality of Diagnostic Examinations in a University Hospital Outpatient Clinic." *Annals of Internal Medicine* 78(1973): 481–489.

A retrospective analysis of patient records and a complete re-examination of selected patients were performed in order to assess the quality of diagnostic evaluations. Records of 249 patients were graded, using a standardized evaluation form and a weighted scoring system. A normal distribution of scores was found. Twenty-five patients from the low-scoring group (130 points or less from a total possible score of 210) were matched for sex, age, and race, with 25 patients in the high-scoring group (170 points or more), and these individuals were completely re-evaluated by a Board-certified internist.

The record analysis showed that, once recognized, abnormalities were almost always further evaluated; however, many procedures defined by the investigators as essential to adequate history, physical examination, and laboratory tests were not systematically performed. A high score was found to be associated with evaluation in more than one clinic and/or with frequent medical visits. Scores were not related to age, race, or sex.

In the 50 patients undergoing thorough re-examination, there were many new and different findings in previously evaluated categories for both the low- and the high-scoring groups. But the total of all new and different findings was 10 times higher for the low-scoring group, largely because of findings in areas which were not recorded as having been evaluated although they might have been.

Comment: In terms of actual improvement of outcome, however, only 2 patients had new therapy and only 13 were followed more closely.

Russo, R. M.; Gururaj, V. J.; Laude, T. A.; Rajkumar, S. V.; and Ventre, S. A. "A Chart Audit Peer Review System in an Ambulatory Service." *Pediatrics* 56(1975): 246–254.

A system of chart audit was developed in a pediatric outpatient service. Twenty-six of the most common primary diagnoses were selected for review, and criteria for them were developed by the committee. Criteria were: integral to diagnosis, acceptable to providers, able to be met by the health facility, applicable to most patients presenting with the conditions, and few (an average of five per disease entity) in number. Of the 196 criteria developed for the 26 conditions, 68 were historical, 60 involved the physical examination, 32 were laboratory-related, and 36 were therapy-related.

The following data were collected:
1)   time required to review records (1 person-minute/chart);
2)   the number and percent of reviewable records;
3)   the number and type of deficiencies identified;
4)   provider compliance with criteria and change in compliance over time; and
5)   the number of correctable chart deficiencies.

Deficiencies were related most often to physical examination and least often to therapeutic management. Physician compliance with audit criteria did not improve over five months.

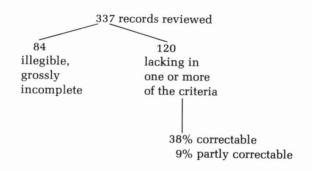

Hulka, B. S.; Kupper, L. L.; and Cassel, J. C. "Physician Management in Primary Care." *American Journal of Public Health* 66(1976): 1173–1179.

Minimal process criteria were set by primary care physicians for four conditions as follows:

APPENDIX A
Components of Management Scores

I. **Infancy**
Instructions

Condition at birth

Feeding schedule

Formula

Frequency

Adding foods

Need for immunizations

How to get emergency care

Baby's weight

Baby's development

Frequency of return visits

Multivitamins
recommended

Physical Examination

	Recorded
	at least
Weight }	3 times
Length }	during
	study
	period

Immunizations

Polio (3 doses)
DPT (3 doses)

II. **Pregnancy**
Instructions

Expected date of confinement

Weight control

Salt restriction

Calorie restriction

Nutritionally adequate diet

Name of hospital for delivery

How to get emergency care

What to do about cramping or bleeding

Frequency of return visits

Physical Examination

Clinical pelvimetry
Presentation of fetus
Fetal heart rate—last trimester
Blood } 2nd and
  pressure } 3rd tri-
Weight } mester
Preeclampsia—if present, evidence of Rx

Laboratory

Urinalysis—2nd and 3rd trimester
Serology
Pap smear
Hgb or Hct
ABO blood type
Rh
Coombs Test in last trimester for Rh negative women

III.   **Diabetes Mellitus**
    Instructions

      Spacing/regularity of food intake

      Weight control

      How to get emergency care

      Frequency of return visits

      Symptoms of hypoglycemia

      What to do about hypoglycemia

      What to do about infec-
        tion, illness, or vomiting

      Urine testing for sugar

      Care of feet

      Urine testing for acetone

      Carry diabetic identification

      Type of syringe

      Rotating injection sites

Physical Examination

Weight
Blood pressure

Laboratory

Urine or blood test for sugar

IV.   **Congestive Heart Failure**
    Instructions

      Diet—low fat

      Diet—low salt

      Activity limitation

      How to get emergency
        care

      Frequency of return
        visits

Physical Examination

Blood
  pressure
Weight or
  edema   } Recorded at least 2 times during study period
Exam of
  heart
Exam of
  lungs

The criteria strongly emphasize personal, prevention-oriented instructions with only a few key physical exam and laboratory test criteria.

For 34 family physicians, 11 internists, 8 pediatricians and 8 obstetricians, scores on the criteria for 1,258 encounters ranged from 78–93%. Pediatricians and obstetricians did somewhat better in their specialty than the family physicians.

Brook, R. H., and Williams, K. N. "Evaluation of the New Mexico Peer Review System—1971 to 1973." Santa Monica, Calif.: Rand Corporation, 1976.

The Experimental Medical Care Review Organization (EMCRO) of New Mexico, acting as a PSRO in tandem with a Medicaid fiscal intermediary, established a peer review system for both in- and outpatient claims. In its first two years some important findings were made:

1. Virtually all denials of payment were for administrative rather than medical reasons, saving 6.7 million dollars (15% of billings).
2. Peer review identified inappropriate injections for payment denial. Their use per visit fell from 40% to 5% of all visits, saving 0.9 million dollars. Since the cost of peer review was 0.5 million, net savings were $400,000 (1% of total billed).
3. Six percent of the physicians were responsible for 40% of the inappropriate injections. Most of these doctors were osteopaths without specialty certification.
4. The structure of PSROs may be useful as the source of review, technical information and professional accountability in the future.

Miller, D. G. "Internal Quality of Care Assessment." In *Insights and Issues: A Volume of Selected Proceedings from a National Series of Conferences for Neighborhood Health Center Medical Directors,* edited by W. J. Manseau, pp. 139–157. Washington, D.C.: National Association of Neighborhood Health Centers, 1975.

Explicit criteria for diagnosis, therapy and follow-up were developed for 13 illnesses and completeness of data-base in an ambulatory care setting. Audit of 900 charts of regular patients (3/physician/month, or 2% of total regular clients) from 1969 to 1972 showed the following compliances with standards:

	Full-time MDs	**Part-time MDs**
Diagnostic	66%	54%
Therapeutic	73%	65%
Follow-up	66%	46%

With an increase in patient load in 1971–1972 adherence to diagnostic standards (full-time MDs) fell from 71 to 57%. This was called a "decrease in the quality of care" in spite of increased utilization.

The audits had little value in changing medical practice. One critical use of the evaluations, however, was *political*. When the data were presented to the board of trustees, they were so impressed by the notion of physicians' publishing the results of self-monitoring that they gave "unflinching support . . . in an attempt to improve quality."

Outcomes

Williamson, J. W. "Outcome Assessment for Implementing Quality Assurance Systems." In *Quality Assurance of Medical Care* (Regional Medical Programs Service: DHEW Monograph, February 1973).

Williamson outlines the variety of outcome measurements:
I. Clinical
    A. Diagnostic
        Percent false negative (missed diagnoses)
    B. Therapeutic
        Impairment (scale of 0-6, no impairment to death)
    C. Economic
        Costs of diagnosis/benefits

	Gradations of outcome
Final:	"Stroke," age 52
Determinants:	Hypertension, noncompliant, stress, family history
Intermediate Outcome:	Didn't take medications
Determinants of Intermediate Outcome:	Didn't understand, no medications, no follow-up.

Method:
1. Identify maximum acceptable impairment by group-at-risk for particular illness in time-degree terms (10% will be impaired at three months, for example).
2. Measure outcome by patient group follow-up.
3. Compare 1. and 2.
4. If 2. worse than 1., study process.
5. If 2. better than 1., go on to next problem.

Method is *group-oriented* (patient group, provider group), forces prognosis (? locally determined ? national/regional standards), allows for comparison of large institutions (coronary care unit A versus coronary care unit B), and picks up at least gross errors.

"Evaluation of the Albemarle EMCRO." Cambridge, Mass.: Arthur D. Little, Inc., for Department of Health, Education and Welfare, Contract HSM 110-73-526, 1974.

A review of the Albemarle EMCRO (West Virginia) effort to establish "validated" process-outcome criteria (based on literature review and prospective research) for hypertension, hip fracture, gastric ulcer, otitis media, myocardial infarction, bacterial pneumonia, urinary tract infection, and appendicitis. Panels of experts assembled for each condition. Only four completed the task:
1. gastric ulcer: studied the yields of common diagnostic procedures;
2. hypertension and hip fracture: literature review and local studies on selected procedures; and
3. otitis media: distinguished between proved procedures and unsupported opinion (use of decongestants).

Medical practice in the case of hypertension was studied, pre- and post-criteria development and education of local physicians: charting actually deteriorated but screening, follow-up and more intense therapy increased. The total effort so far cost $200,000.

   Comment: The results for hypertension suggest a "Hawthorne" effect (that is, merely paying attention to a topic increases activity in it); more intense therapy may or may not improve outcomes. The result of the otitis media study—not to use decongestants—is trivial in relation to outcome.

Zimmer, M. J.; Lang, N. M.; and Miller, D. I. "Development of Sets of Patient Health Outcome Criteria by Panels of Nurse Experts." Wisconsin Regional Medical Program, University of Wisconsin Hospitals Nursing Service, University of Wisconsin–Milwaukee School of Nursing, 1974.

This set of outcome criteria was developed by and for nurses.

Unlike most criteria employed by physicians, these specify functional physical and psychological outcomes that:

1. are controllable by medical/nursing care; and
2. make a big difference to the individual patient's well-being.

The conditions chosen were:

Chronic obstructive pulmonary disease

Cerebro-vascular accident in a nursing home

Psychogenic depression

Acute recurrent otitis media

Systemic immobilization

Normal first pregnancy

Hypertension

All criteria were categorized and scaled 1–3 or 1–4 on levels of patient activity, or body measurements, or patient-awareness of condition, treatment, and prevention. Samples are given below of criteria scaling.

Comment: While testing is still needed, the criteria strongly suggest that nursing, caring, and preventive aspects of medical care, especially for chronic or recurrent disease, are critical factors in the quality of care.

Criteria for Outcome in Chronic Obstructive Pulmonary Disease

1. Maintenance of clear airway.
2. Control of dyspnea.
3. Maintenance of activity.
4. Maintenance of adequate nutrition.
5. Maintenance of adequate hydration.
6. Freedom from acute infections.
7. Psycho-social adjustment to regimen.
8. Maintenance of environment (include equipment).
9. Ability to adhere to prescribed home care regime.

CRITERION 3: MAINTAINS ACTIVITIES

Scale #1:

1	2	3	4
Unable to perform activities of daily living (ADL) (feed, toilet, dress, bathe).	Performs ADL with assistance.	Performs some ADL independently.	Performs all ADL independently.

Scale #2:

1	2	3	4
Unable to plan or pursue activities other than ADL.	Pursues activities (other than ADL) by others.	Able to plan and pursue activities (other than ADL) with assistance.	Independently plans and pursues activities (other than ADL).

CRITERION 6: FREEDOM FROM ACUTE INFECTIOUS EXACERBATIONS

Scale #1:

1	2	3	4
Free for one month of acute infection requiring hospitalization.	Free for six months of acute infection requiring hospitalization.	Free for one year of acute infection requiring hospitalization.	Maintains self, free of acute infectious exacerbation requiring hospitalization.

Scale #2:

1	2	3	4
Does not use prescribed Bronchial Hygiene Regime (BHR) (including care of equipment).	Uses prescribed BHR sporadically or intermittently.	Uses prescribed BHR on daily basis.	Performs and adjusts prescribed BHR as necessary.

Scale #3:

1	2	3	4
Does not inspect sputum.	Inspects sputum but does not recognize change in pattern.	Inspects sputum, recognizes changes, does not take appropriate action.	Inspects sputum daily for quantity, color, consistency and recognizes change in pattern and takes appropriate action.

Mushlin, A. I.; Appel, F. A.; Pozen, J. T.; Zauber, A. G.; and Koch, J. F. "The Use of Patient-Reported Problem Status in Evaluating Ambulatory Care." Columbia, Md.: Johns Hopkins Health Services Research and Development Center; presented at the National Meeting of the American Federation for Clinical Research, 3 May 1975.

This study documents outcome status as reported by the patient for a specific problem in terms of frequency and intensity of symptoms, degree of activity limitation, and anxiety all tested initially and one month later. The technique requires a high degree of follow-up and client compliance. The three conditions studied were viral sore throat (VST), upper respiratory infection (URI), and urinary tract infection (UTI). Outcome criteria: After one month patient should report no symptoms, no limitation of activity, no anxiety.

	VST	URI	UTI
Percent *not* meeting outcome criteria:	8%	32%	25%

Thirty-five percent of those not meeting the criteria had comorbid or relevant factors that could complicate outcomes (against 9% of those who did meet the criteria).

The proportion of patients with inadequate diagnostic work-up or inadequate treatment was the same in the groups with good or bad outcomes. Initial diagnosis was more often incorrect (25% vs. 3% of cases; 1 vs. 5) in the poor-outcome group. However, most of the misdiagnoses were for mononucleosis, which has its own course whether diagnosed or not.

By implicit review:

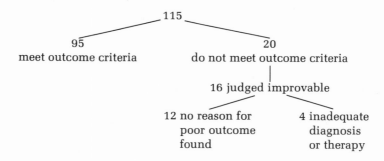

Comment: VST and URI are generally trivial, self-limited conditions; by the nature of the follow-up, an artificially high degree of patient complaints of anxiety may have been fostered; where patient-reported outcomes were unsatisfactory, most have nothing to do with the process of care.

"The Development and Testing of Methods and Procedures to Assess and Assure the Delivery of Quality Personal Health Care." Columbia, Maryland: Management Advisory Services, Inc., 1974.

This is an unpublished report applying outcome measurements of tracer conditions in two health centers, one urban and one rural. Taking hypertension, diabetes, tonsillitis, urinary tract infection (based on a profile of the centers' practice, these represented a total of 12–16% of the patient population), criteria were developed for process (history and physical, performance of lab tests and diagnosis treatment, follow-up). Equal weights were given to each of the four process categories (complete adherence = 1, majority complete = 0.5, majority incomplete = 0). Outcomes were measured by stages (worse, better, no longer a problem).

X^2 tests for pre- and post-protocol outcomes gave a measure of improvement in the same group of patients (first center) or two groups of patients (second center).

Significant improvements, at a 10% confidence level, were found for the first center for 3/4 conditions and 0/4 at the second center.

As a result of the audit the *first* center set up appointment schedules for different types of care (uncomplicated maintenance, complicated maintenance) and an outreach program.

Comment:
1. the center showing improvement in outcomes also made process changes, suggesting a dynamic commitment to improvement that might have occurred anyway;
2. the expression of improvement by statistics gives no absolute sense of magnitude, and there are no "controls"—patients may have been getting better anyway;

3.   the exercise was costly and time-consuming; and
4.   outcomes assessment is a good community status tool.

Schroeder, S. A., and Donaldson, M. S. "The Feasibility of an Outcome Approach to Quality Assurance—A Report from One HMO." *Medical Care* 14(1976): 49–56.

In an inner-city HMO, audits of three conditions (contraception, depression, hypertension) were made, and diagnostic outcomes (% missed) and therapeutic outcomes (% improved on functional scale) were measured. This outcome audit technique is based on Williamson's Health Accounting method. Missed diagnoses (false negative) were present in all three in about 50%, and therapeutic outcomes were unacceptable for depression and hypertension by a wide margin. High mobility of clients, disenrollment, and insensitivity (or difficulty in application) of the functional scale make use of data to improve outcomes unlikely.

Access, outreach and compliance may be more important to look at than simply process and therapeutic outcomes.

Hare, R. "Assessment of Performance." In *The Changing Health Care Team: Improving Effectiveness in Patient Care*, edited by S. Zoog and S. Yarnall. Seattle, Washington: Medical Communications and Services Association, 1976.

The American Society of Internal Medicine has pilot studies in two clusters of private practice which attempt to define measurable process and outcome components of care for specific illnesses. A sample of a developed protocol is given in the following figure.

ASPERF CRITERIA FOR
URINARY TRACT INFECTION

PROCESS AND OUTCOME EVALUATION AREAS	EXPECTED DOCUMENTATION AND OUTCOMES
1. HISTORY PHYSICAL	1. DYSURIA-FREQUENCY URGENCY-HEMATURIA
2. PROBLEM IDENTIFICATION	2. URINARY TRACT DYSFUNCTION
3. INVESTIGATIVE MANAGEMENT	3. URINALYSIS URINE CULTURE
4. PROBLEM RESOLUTION	4. URINARY TRACT INFECTION
5. THERAPEUTIC MANAGEMENT	5. ANTIBACTERIAL AGENT
6. MANAGEMENT (SHORT TERM)	6. RELIEF OF SYMPTOMS WITHIN 72 HOURS
7. CONTINUING CARE	7. POST-TREATMENT CULTURE
8. MANAGEMENT GOAL (LONG TERM)	8. BACTERIOLOGICAL CURE

No data on efficacy of this approach are given, two years after its inception. The author says, "We remain very much impressed with the difficulty and the magnitude of the task of evaluating the quality of medical care."

Starfield, B. "Measurements of Outcome: A Proposed Scheme." *Milbank Memorial Fund Quarterly*, Health and Society: Winter (1974) 39–50.

Another view of outcome attributes on a nominal, non-interval scale:
1.   resilience (ability to cope with adversity):
         resilient or vulnerable;
2.   achievement (cognitive, motor, mental):
         achieving or non-achieving;
3.   disease:
         not detectable, asymptomatic, temporary, permanent;
4.   satisfaction:
         yes or no;
5.   comfort:
         yes or no;
6.   activity:
         functional or disabled;
7.   longevity:
         normal expectancy or dead.
The author suggests research to develop an outcome profile to find quantitative indicator points for each attribute.

Richman, A., and Pinkser, H. "Medical Audit by Clinical Rounds." *American Journal of Psychiatry* 131(1974): 1370–1374.

Even in psychiatry, where outcomes are difficult to evaluate, simple indicators of proximate outcomes can be found:
1.   delays in using shock therapy;
2.   use of medications;
3.   referrals;
4.   readmissions;
5.   access; and
6.   discharge.

Grogono, A. W., and Woodgate, D. J. "Index for Measuring Health." *Lancet* 2(1971): 1024–1026.

This is a sample of one of several health indices: it scales ten indicators by 0, 0.5, and 1.0.

work
recreation
physical pain
mental pain
communication
sleep
dependency
feeding
excretion
sexual activity

Like other similar indices, components are not really independent; but this one is easy to construct as a proximate outcome measure for individual patients.

McClure, W. *Background Paper II on the Technical Feasibility of Regulating Medical Care by Outcomes.* Springfield, Va.: National Technical Information Services, PB256 222, 1972.

This paper suggests establishment of a Health Outcomes Commission to regulate the quality of care of federally funded Health Maintenance Organizations by technical assistance, provision of data, and supervision and sanctions. The author strictly recommends one of the following outcome measures to assess quality:
1. *high-priority proximate outcomes* (85% of appendectomies should show inflamed appendix; x% of hypertension should be under control);
2. *Williamson's clinical outcomes approach* (required levels of diagnostic inaccuracy and therapeutic success); or
3. *Brook's mixed process-outcome method* (minimal process criteria, following of patients to determine match of good and bad outcomes, good and bad process).

All methods require the following steps:
a)   list all problems by estimated priority;

b) consider the first problem: set ideal and minimum acceptable pattern performance standards by estimation;
c) have allied personnel collect and display performance
compared to standards;
d) if performance is below standard, make detailed investigation into structural and medical processes. If performance is above standard, go on to next problem;
e) if shown necessary, recommend and implement corrective action;
f) proceed to next problem;
g) at specified later date, reassess any previous below-stan-
dard performance on first problem. Take further corrective steps until performance is satisfactory; and
h) periodically revise priorities and standards.

The Health Outcomes Commission would enforce the measurement and assurance of quality outcomes by setting guidelines,
providing help, requiring annual reports, conducting on-site in-
spections (announced and unannounced), providing incentives
(the HOC "Seal of Approval" to be displayed prominently on the
HMO front door; federal monies), and sanctions (after continued
failure to meet guidelines):
1.   mandatory recommendations;
2.   on site "observer-advisors";
3.   fines;
4.   disqualification from federal monies;
5.   replacement of HMO management "in favor of HOC appointed rehabilitation"; and
6.   revocation of the right to operate.

Williamson, J. W. "Formulating Priorities for Quality Assurance
Activity. Description of a Method and Its Application." *JAMA*
239(1978): 631–637.

The author has followed quality assessment activities in 23
multispecialty group clinics for 14 years. He recommends a sophisticated method for choosing priority topics of care to assess whose

processes can and should improve outcomes. In order to do this a core team of seven is selected (four physicians), and the nominal group process is taught and used to select topics for assessment. A comprehensive literature source is used to provide evidence on health care efficacy and the likely impact of correcting deficits (Williamson's own annotated bibliography is recommended: "Improving Medical Practice and Health Care: A Bibliographic Guide to Information Management in Quality Assurance and Continuing Education." Cambridge, Mass.: Ballinger, 1977). After topics are selected, the Executive Board selects the final list, and a special study team is appointed for each topic. The stress is on determining where achievable benefits have not been achieved. In 14 years the 23 groups identified 233 topics, of which 77 were selected for study and 74 were completed: 0.23 topics/practice/year.

Sample topics were:

1.   "Follow-up evaluation by internists of occupational rehabilitation of male postmyocardial infarction patients 40 to 50 years of age";
2.   "Better patient follow-up by physician assistants to check condition of any postsurgical and postpartum patients with any health problem";
3.   "Group counseling by physicians, nurse practitioners, or health educators for better self-care of adults with chronic heart disease";
4.   "Adult education by nutritionists for parents of children from birth to 10 years of age with poor nutrition";
5.   "Identification of patients with sexual dysfunction by primary care physicians";
6.   "Treatment of parenting problems by primary care practitioners and mental health therapists";
7.   "More specific diagnosis of learning disorders by physicians and school psychologists in school-age children";
8.   "Review of therapy, follow-up therapy, and education by physicians, nurses, and health educators for unwanted pregnancy in adolescent and adult females";
9.   "Counseling by all physicians for depression in tired housewives."; and
10. "Clinic staff arrangement for decreased exposure of well-baby pediatric patients to acute illness in the waiting room."

Over 14 years topics moved away from single organic medical diseases to multiple illnesses and social issues; from treatment to prevention and screening; and from physician behavior to patient and administrative behavior.

The author promises further papers documenting the success of this method.

Tracers

Kessner, D. M., and Kalk, C. E. "A Strategy for Evaluating Health Services." Washington, D.C.: Institute of Medicine, National Academy of Sciences, 1972.

The authors review "tracer" methodology; they start from the premise that adequate processes for and outcomes of several diseases will stand for overall quality of care. The attributes of a tracer should be:
1. easy to diagnose;
2. highly prevalent;
3. having a significant functional impact;
4. having a proven substantial impact on medical care;
5. having a consensus on criteria for management; and
6. having an understood epidemiology.
Six conditions meet these attributes:
1. otitis media;
2. visual disorders;
3. iron-deficiency anemia;
4. urinary tract infections;
5. cervical cancer; and
6. hypertension.
The tracer method measures both process and outcome. Minimal and pragmatic criteria for tracer diagnosis and management were formulated with the expectation of periodic revision and updating. An implicit assumption is the need for good medical records.

Kessner, D. M.; Singer, J.; and Snow, C. K. *Assessing Ambulatory Care: The Use of an Enriched Encounter Form.* Springfield, Va.: National Technical Information Services, 1975.

This method is designed for small practices through the use of enriched encounter forms. The encounter forms, processed by computer, link a number of data items:
1.   age;
2.   sex;
3.   chief complaint;
4.   diagnosis/problems and severity;
5.   lab tests, x-rays and procedures;
6.   drug therapy; and
7.   follow-up plan and outside referral.

The technique can sample encounters from a random several-day segment or from a large block of time. The sample should use "tracer" diseases which reflect common local conditions that ordinarily call for some or all of the data items on the encounter form. (In this study hypertension, anemia, depression, and urinary tract infection were used.) Minimal care criteria for the conditions, including *unacceptable* practices, assist in auditing the forms.

The stress of the audit is maximal improvability, convenience and low cost.

The results of the study:
1.   there were 9,000 encounters from six sites;
2.   the four tracers accounted for about 15% of the diagnoses;
3.   a) less than 50% of those with anemia were untreated or given inappropriate agents;
     b) 1/6 of moderate hypertension and 1/10 of severe hypertension were untreated;
     c) 1/3 of the neurotically depressed patients got insufficient treatment;
     d) over 40% of patients getting digitalis and a diuretic had no supplemental potassium;
     e) in 15% of the patients getting reserpine, depression was present;
     f) over 50% of the diagnosed urinary tract infections had no urine cultures; and
     g) over 75% of patients with anxiety had insufficient follow-up.

The cost of audit was $2.60 per encounter form (prorated over all visits, it was considerably lower).

Novick, L. F.; Dickinson, K.; Asnes, R.; May Lan, S. P.; and Lowenstein, R. "Assessment of Ambulatory Care: Application of Tracer Methodology." *Medical Care* 14(1976): 1–12.

A study was undertaken to evaluate care for iron-deficiency anemia by means of the tracer technique. Twenty-two explicit criteria were developed concerning the evaluation, diagnosis, treatment, and follow-up of pediatric patients suspected of having iron-deficiency anemia. One hundred cases were chosen for record review. Assessment was carried out by non-physicians using a weighted scoring system. The sample was then reviewed by a physician panel using implicit peer review. Of the 100 suspected cases, only 25 proceeded through all levels of care and kept scheduled follow-up appointments. In 52 of the 100 cases, a low hemoglobin level was not recognized. Poor provider compliance was found with explicit criteria. The mean time spent on assessment by non-physicians was 5.1 minutes; for physicians, it was 3.9 minutes. Limitations of the tracer method are dependence on good medical records, on accurate diagnoses, and on a possibly nonexistent relationship between process and outcome, and the complexity of tracking back through a complete medical system.

Sibley, J. C. "Indicator Conditions for Development of a Quality of Care Appraisal Method for Primary Health Care Projects." McMaster University, Division of Health Sciences, 1972.

The audit method developed at McMaster University combines several approaches. It:
1.   uses "tracer" conditions:

     otitis media;   urinary tract infections
     hypertension;   in women over 16;
     prenatal care;   knee trauma;
     well-baby care;   anemia;
     immunization;   pityriasis rosea; and
     depression;   drug use;

2.   uses the "staging concept," classification by severity in some illnesses (hypertension, depression, urinary tract infection);
3.   lists absolute minimal intervention criteria for "adequate" care and extra criteria for "superior care" (often in a psychosocial area); and
4.   provides options for criteria (not all items necessary for all people). Criteria are grouped by history, physical, diagnostic, therapy and referral/follow-up.

Sibley, J. C.; Spitzer, W. O.; Rudnick, K. V.; Bell, J. D.; Bethune, R. D.; Sackett, D. L.; and Wright, K. "Quality-of-Care Appraisal in Primary Care: A Quantitative Method." *Annals of Internal Medicine* 83(1975): 46–52.

An expansion of explicit process and tracer methodologies to measure adequacy of nurse practitioner practice:
Process I
    Indicator Conditions
        Otitis
        Hypertension
        Prenatal Care
        Newborn Care
        Immunization 1st Year
        Depression
        Urinary Tract Infection
        Knee Injury
        Pityriasis
        Anemia
    Explicit Criteria:
        Essential monitoring of data base
        No major errors
        No missed diagnosis
Process II
    Satisfactory use and non-use of 13 common drugs
Process III
    Judicious referral

Adequate or superior practice were assessed about 70% of the time for each process, slightly better for nurses than for MDs. The cost of such an audit can be high.

The study demonstrates: the choice of several independent measurements that are likely to stand as reasonable surrogates for something called "quality."

Dreyfus, E. G.; Minson, R.; Sbararo, J. A.; and Cowen, D. L. "Internal Chart Audits in a Neighborhood Health Program: A Problem-Oriented Approach." *Medical Care* 9(1971).

A major obstacle to the provision of good medical care in neighborhood health centers and other ambulatory care settings is the episodic nature of care. Resistance to chart audits was encountered in this health center network; chart documentation was argued to have no bearing on the care actually given.

A topical approach to chart audit was developed following the discovery of a potentially unsound prescribing pattern. Providers participated in establishing explicit criteria suitable for this setting. The goal of the audit was to select significant problems that could be studied quickly, in a sample of 40–50 charts, with the hope of producing a composite picture of the group's practice. The first audit was of indomethacin prescriptions; the second of hypertension.

Follow-up showed: a 25% reduction in the indomethacin dispensed, and a drug cost reduction of $1,000 per year; and more thorough work-ups and more consultation for hypertensive patients. Each audit used two hours of provider time. Greatest benefit was seen in the use of the audit as continuing education.

Kessner, D. M. "Quality Assessment and Assurance: Early Signs of Cognitive Dissonance." *The New England Journal of Medicine* 298(1978): 381–386.

The author has become disillusioned with methods of assessing quality of care, including his own—the tracer method. Defeating most attempts are: inconsistent record-keeping; lack of diagnostic specificity; misdiagnoses; likely differences from one practice to another in the prevalence of common conditions; poor voluntary compliance by physicians; and little connection between process and outcome. The costs of assessment (direct ones and those produced by generating more processes of care) must be determined.

Staging

McCord, J.; Cattani, J.; and Louis, D. *The Staging Methodology: A System for Analyzing the Quality, Outcome and Cost of Medical Care.* Santa Barbara, Calif.: SysteMetrics, Inc., 1976.

The staging concept is based on the assumption that "the seriousness of a patient's condition at a given point in the process of care reflects the outcome of previous parts of the process," whether physician-, environment-, or self-induced. Nearly all important illnesses can be "staged."

Stage 1 = "no complications, or problems of minimal severity";

Stage 2 = local complications or problems of moderate severity; and

Stage 3 = condition with systemic complications or problems of a serious nature.

Staging has been done for 40 conditions which account for 35% of hospital admissions and 25% of ambulatory care patients. The criteria for stages are:

1. usefulness of medical intervention;
2. a well-understood progression of illness;
3. sufficient incidence;
4. ready diagnosis; and involvement of all parts of the care system.

Example:

Hypertension (untreated)

Stage I   A.   Diastolic $\leq$ 100
          B.   Diastolic $\leq$ 120

Stage II   Diastolic > 120

Stage III   Hypertension plus complication

Diabetes

Stage I   —Chemical diagnosis (tolerance test or fasting)

Stage II   —Diagnosis plus infection, acidosis or end-organ disease

Stage III   —Severe end-organ disease

The major applications of the staging method are testing of outcomes, comparison of client groups, comparison of costs of care, and identification of process-of-performance problems in care. (See sample attached.)

1.   In actual test of program effectiveness it was found that county welfare patients (mostly migrants with poor access to care) were at higher stages than insured or pre-paid clients. Similar findings occurred for blacks vs. whites. Comparison of comprehensive health centers' clients with people of similar socio-economic background who used other sources of care showed very little difference in stage prevalence.

2.   Staging can also track population trends in illness over time.

3.   In order to detect program difficulties, stage prevalence must be compared to another site or another time.

4.   Cost analysis shows increased (2–3x) cost for medical care between stages for hospital conditions; the technique will allow for cost-benefit analyses.

5.   There is a *slight* suggestion that early diagnosis reduces the prevalence of Stage III, but not spectacularly.

6.   Undesirable outcomes (Stage III) can be tagged and the record backtracked to find problems in process (client- or provider-related). Process should be tailored to each stage.

Assurance or remedial action, however, still depends on providing provider knowledge, client access and education, follow-up and a proper "treatment environment."

Comment:

The main features of staging are that it:

1.   provides attention to gross errors as outcomes;

2.   is useful in inter-group, inter-time comparisons;

3.   forces process decisions to be logically suited to stage;

4.   is cheap, record-based;

5.   requires excellent follow-up and record linkages to hospital;

6.   becomes unclear for clients with two or more conditions (Diabetes, Stage I; Hypertension, Stage II) when priorities are needed; interactions of diseases and remedies not considered;

7.   always needs a control population (actual or ideal); and

8.   rarely provides auditing for minor, acute problems.

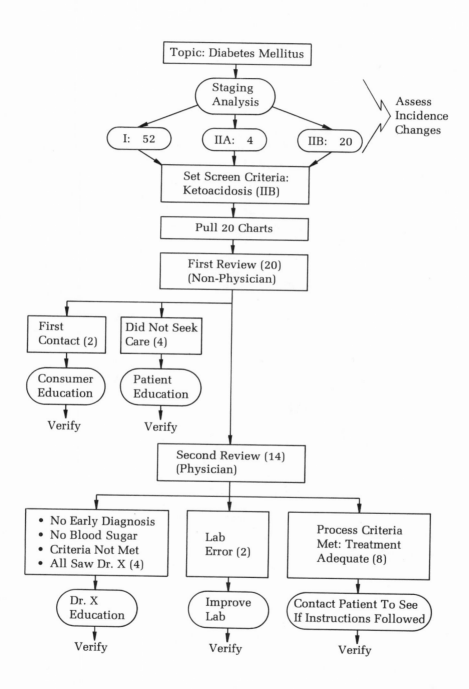

Criteria Mapping

Greenfield, S.; Lewis, C. E.; Kaplan, S. H.; and Davidson, M. B.
"Peer Review by Criteria Mappings: Criteria for Diabetes Mellitus
—The Use of Decision-Making in Chart Audit." *Annals of Internal
Medicine* 83(1975): 761–770.

In view of the limitations of peer review using explicit criteria, the UCLA EMCRO has developed a retrospective medical audit system called "criteria mapping." In this system, criteria are developed to reflect sequential medical decision-making based on the specific findings for the individual patients. The example used is the criteria map for diabetes mellitus which contains a total of 133 individual criteria. Criteria are developed by specialists and are presented in three components: the Physician's Map (P-Map), a written description of the criteria items grouped according to objectives for care (e.g., diagnosis, screening for complications, and management); the Abstractor's Map (A-Map), a branching flow diagram derived from the P-Map; and the Abstraction Guidelines, which provide complete definitions of criteria. One purpose of the maps is to avoid penalizing the physician for omitting unnecessary procedures; e.g., for diabetes, there are four alternate ways to arrive at a diagnosis—all are accepted, and only one is required.

In a study reviewing 30 charts, nonprofessional abstracters used a mean of 25 minutes per chart, had more than a 90% accuracy rate, and found a mean of 13.7 criteria items (of 133) to be applicable. Using this method, unrealistic criteria have been identified and eliminated. Twenty percent of the charts have been identified as deficient and have required physician review. Advantages of this system are patient-sensitivity and institution-specificity; limitations include lack of validated criteria, problems of nonrecording, and technical difficulty in constructing the maps.

Greenfield, S.; Nadler, M. A.; Morgan, M. T.; and Shine, K. I. "The Clinical Investigation and Management of Chest Pain in an Emergency Department: Quality Assessment by Criteria Mapping." *Medical Care* 15(1977): 898–905.

A criteria map for the complaint of chest pain was developed and tested on 137 patients who were examined for chest pain in an emergency room and either admitted or discharged.

The criteria map is intended to be a blueprint of good medical logic, following sequential, branching steps based on successive bits of information, and can be designed to address a *presenting problem*, rather than a diagnosis. Tables 1 and 2 give some of the logic and examples of *critical* criteria.

TABLE 1. FIRST SECTION OF CHEST PAIN CRITERIA MAP

I. If chest pain is excruciating and unremitting, admit . . .

II. A. Check for the presence of any of the following:
  1. cold clammy skin
  2. gray or cyanotic skin
  3. hypotension:
   Female <25: BP<80/60
   Female >25: BP<100/60
   Male   >20: BP<100/60
 B. If any of the above is present, admit . . .

III. If there is difficulty inhaling, and either acroparesthesias or circumoral paresthesias, and patient is male <30 or female <40, discharge.

IV. Do EKG.

V. If EKG reveals any of the following that are not proven old, admit . . .
  1. unifocal premature ventricular contractions x 10/minute;
  2. back-to-back premature ventricular contractions;
  3. multifocal premature ventricular contractions;
  4. R-wave on T-wave;
  5. ventricular tachycardia; and
  6. second- or third-degree heart block.

Table 2. Examples of Critical Criteria (Requiring Admission)

Any of the following:

cold, clammy skin;

gray, cyanotic skin;

hypotension: Females <25: BP<80/60;
             Females >25: BP<100/60;
             Males   >20: BP<100/60;

excruciating or unremitting pain;

dyspnea or diffuse precordial pain over 20 minutes in patients over 45.

If:
1.   Symptoms of tamponade are present, *or*
2.   Chest x-ray shows enlarged heart shadow or abnormal contour, *or*
3.   Small effusion is present on ECHO cardiogram, or a 3-component rub is present, *unless* patient has a history of recurrent pericarditis.

"Good process" means appropriately admitted to hospital, or not, according to the criteria map. Twenty-six in 137 were inadequate (19%), with poor outcomes in 3/26:

	Good outcome	Poor outcome
Good process	111	0
Poor process	23	3

(significantly different)

    105 were hospitalized justifiably:
        43% had a heart attack
        21% had other acute coronary artery disease
        26% had no specific diagnosis but all had signs or symptoms that made an acute event highly possible
        11% had a serious noncardiac condition.

Brook, R. H.; Avery, A. D.; Greenfield, S.; Harris, L. J.; Lelah, T.; Solomon, N. E.; and Ware, J. E., Jr. *Quality of Medical Care Assessment Using Outcome Measures.* Santa Monica, Calif.: The Rand Corporation, 1976.

The Rand Corporation identified eight diseases or surgical procedures whose early or proximate outcomes directly reflect good process, thereby overcoming the usual objections to outcome assessment of: time-lag, scant relationship to medical process, dependency on client compliance, dependency on large populations with a particular disease, etc. These eight conditions were: asthma; breast mass; cholecystectomy; diarrhea and dehydration in children; ischemic heart disease; osteoarthrosis; otitis media in children; tonsillectomy. The eight conditions are a mix of inpatient, outpatient, medical, surgical and emergency conditions across a wide age spectrum. Eight panels of experts balanced in perspective (epidemiologic, clinical, teaching, etc.), assisted by extensive literature reviews, assembled proximate *outcome* criteria by a modified Delphi technique (feeding back initial group results to individual experts in private for re-evaluation in order to derive a consensus). None of the criteria so established was validated in this phase.

The study considered only two uses for outcome auditing: to affect area-wide policy (systems, deployment, funding) and for in-house medical monitoring. The management or organizational aspect was not discussed.

The most important development of this study was the setting of "top-priority outcome standards" which, when translated, reflect gross incompetence or failure of access.

Condition	Top Priority Outcome Standard
ASTHMA	Given 5 stages of severity (A=50% of population with fewer than six mild attacks per year and normal otherwise, D–E=10% with over eight severe attacks on continuous medication), no change in stage prevalence, and only 2% get worse.
BREAST MASS (Cancer)	60–70% with negative nodes on histology at first Rx.
CHOLECYSTECTOMY	Mortality: 0.8% uncomplicated 1.1% with negative bile duct exploration 2.6% with positive bile duct exploration Review *all* deaths

DIARRHEA AND DEHYDRATION	No deaths regardless of severity in any child between the ages of 0 and 2.
ISCHEMIC HEART DISEASE	With antiarrhythmic drugs and CPR, sudden death rate should be reduced to 2–3% with average care; with top flight CCU care, reduced 10–20% (from pre-CPR days).
OSTEOARTHROSIS	90% should improve or stay the same. Confinement to bed calls for surgery.
OTITIS MEDIA	Less than 25% should have 15–40 db hearing loss 3–12 months after episode.
TONSILLECTOMY	No surgery if any contraindications exist; PTT and PT values should be normal and recorded on 99% of chart; any surgery without excellent indication should be investigated.

To develop major criteria costs $30,000 per disease and $250,000 per disease for field valuation of method.

"At this time, it seems appropriate that the major purpose of operational quality assessment programs be the identification of those physicians practicing exceptionally poor medicine."

Microsampling

Rubin, L. *Comprehensive Quality Assurance System: The Kaiser Permanente Approach.* Alexandria, Va.: American Group Practice Association, 1975.

The conceptual bases of the Comprehensive Quality Assurance System (CQAS) are:
1. emphasis on *quality control* of medical care according to set standards rather than cost-containment, or accreditation, or research, etc. The quality control will promote the other objectives, however;
2. stress on improvement by attack on errors of omission and commission; no attempt to derive an "index" of quality;
3. review of a cross section of the entire practice rather than of specific diagnoses;
4. no commitment to one or another form of medical record, but use of all sources (logs, consumer complaints, consultants, etc.) that hint at sub-optimal care;
5. dissection of the multiplicity of elements from entry to system to exit that go into medical care with quantifiable standards written for each element. The standards are "preferred actions for a particular element of care by a particular professional group under a given set of circumstances." The standards are screening devices, signalling a need for further review if not met; and
6. there is no place for "acceptable level" (i.e., some percentage group performance as in health accounting). "Health accounting" sets percent levels of acceptable variations in standards; this is invalid in not pinpointing the cause or origin of the variation; or the average set level may mean over or under performance by the individual members of the group, neither being desirable. CQAS standards are "all-or-none."

The application of CQAS follows the following steps:
1. problem identification (from any source, record or department) by "micro sampling"—all patients seen in the past

155

4–6 weeks at certain hours of certain days (changing the time from audit to audit). Time-frames should be such as to find the maximum number of problems (e.g., Friday 4 P.M. charts). Charts of "no-shows" are often more valuable for picking up errors of omission or commission than other charts. Sources of problems should also include complaint forms, consultant reports, even telephone and triage logs. Twenty records per department per month will reveal enough sub-optimal care to keep everyone busy!;

2. use of unstructured implicit review by provider to pick up big errors (provider- or patient-related) starting with the index visit and then riffling backwards and forwards (inadequate follow-up, uncoordinated care, poor combination or use of medicines, missed lab results, over-utilization, etc.). Emphasis on *what* is wrong, not *who*. Search for records at times of day when errors are most likely;

3. a second reviewer checks findings, looks for additional problems, and negotiates the final report with the first reviewer;

4. the agreed-on reports go to a review committee. Suboptimal care events are discussed by the two reviewers and unanimously agreed on by the peer committee, then become the substrates for standard-setting. (Serious differences of opinion on what sub-optimal care is may signal a need for outside evaluation or consultants);

5. if a patient continues to be at risk from a discovered error, the situation is corrected as soon as possible. Otherwise, no attempt is made to blame individual providers, but the discoveries go into the setting of new standards;

6. standards should be simple, clear statements of performance, problem-directed and flexible, with successive audits. They are statements of goals from which benchmarks are derived to measure improvability of achievements. An example: "All patients over age 40 seen in office will have blood pressure recorded biannually if seen biannually." All standards must be unanimously accepted by the providers affected. Unanimity is reached by passively allowing for negative responses to memoranda (like Government method via Federal Register); and

7. four audit worksheets are used. Worksheet 1 lists the stan-

dard, any modifications, type, source and number of data to be audited;

Worksheet 2 clerically identified charts at variance with the standard and notes any unusual clustering (e.g., one provider's or one department's charts mostly at variance);

Worksheet 3 is a clinical review of each variant with comments and a tally of which variants are justified, which not;

Worksheet 4 is the analysis and action recommended/action taken log sheet.

Characteristics of the method are that it:

1.   uses measurable, targeted standards against which to assess and assure (definition of "quality");
2.   is economical;
3.   has a short lead time, turn-about time;
4.   needs no change in the record system;
5.   has no need for clinical abstracts;
6.   has no need for computers;
7.   is applicable to sites of any size;
8.   uses local standards; and
9.   points out improvement areas or problem areas.

Comment: Major weaknesses are:

1.   a temptation to write trivial, non-controversial standards;
2.   flooding with multiple standards which become hard to keep track of (except by computer; CQAS at Kaiser has over 1,000 targeted standards);
3.   fragmentation of responsibility for standards, especially "systems" standards;
4.   involvement primarily with technical and recorded aspects of care and not with larger organizational or community issues (although this is not necessarily a fault of the CQAS, but of its implementation by the medical staff); and
5.   the actual improvements wrought by the system since 1972 are limited to anecdotal recounting of some "system" improvements (mostly in records and communications), none of which seems major in terms of cost or improved patient outcomes.

Major Error Audit

Jacobs, C. M.; Christoffel, T. H.; and Dixon, N. Chapter 5. In *Measuring the Quality of Patient Care: The Rationale for Outcome Audit*. Cambridge, Mass.: Ballinger Publishing Co., 1976.

This is a review of the method suggested by the Joint Commission on the Accreditation of Hospitals:

1. Select an audit study topic or disease by factors of commonness, severity, and the extent to which process affects outcome.
2. Classify the topic in several ways:
   diagnostic steps,
   admission criteria,
   therapy/procedures,
   outcome status, etc.
3. Match to records' retrievability (or redesign record?).
4. Write the objectives of the audit.
5. Choose the sample.
6. Narrow topically—not "hypertension," but "hypertension in young black males."
7. Select major criteria for: diagnosis; justification for special procedures, for hospitalization, for complications, for discharge (or outcome status); and follow-up.
   CHOOSE ONLY CRITERIA WHICH SHOULD BE 100% (ALWAYS) OR 0% (NEVER) MET, LISTING ONE OR TWO EXCEPTIONS THAT ARE ACCEPTABLE.
   Example:

I. BACTERIAL PNEUMONIA

a. *Diagnostic*	**Standard**	**Exception**
Positive chest x-ray	100%	Diffuse fibrosis with acute symptoms
Positive gram stain and culture	100%	Acute symptoms already on antibiotics

Admission	**Standard**	**Exception**
For respiratory distress, or failure to improve, or sepsis	100%	None
Justification of Procedure		
Pleural tap	0% (Not needed)	*Only* for fluid if course suggests empyema, TB; or for relief of respiratory difficulty
Discharge Status		
Improved	100%	Major complications (septicemia, alcoholism, MI, diabetes, etc.)
Review All Failures		
	100%	None
Follow-Up		
Within 2 weeks	100%	None except mortality, migration
Patient learning	100%	None
Complications		
Respiratory failure	0%	*Critical management* ventilation, continuous volume cycled airway

This "performance evaluation procedure" (PEP) looks at major flows and major flaws in care, stresses minimal process criteria, examines short-term or proximate outcomes, and uses the concept of "critical management."

8.   PEP is less useful for many ambulatory care conditions, except that the technique can be adopted to several elements of care:

   Diagnosis
   Drugs used
   Patient education
   Follow-up
   Complications

9.   Where an audit shows variations, these should be analyzed as follows:

   a.   forgotten exception (criterion list needs revisions);
   b.   rare exception, not listed;
   c.   complex exception (medical, social, personal);
   d.   state-of-the-art exception (*nothing* can be done);
   e.   failure to record;
   f.   failure in structure of care; and
   g.   failure in process of care.

The costs and the timing of the audit are not discussed. The method suffers from a time lag between the actual event or non-event discovery, and repair.

Rutstein, D. D.; Berenberg, W.; Chalmers, T. C.; Child, C. G.; Fishman, A. P.; and Perrin, E. B. "Measuring the Quality of Medical Care." *The New England Journal of Medicine* 294(1976): 582–588.

This article describes an outcome measurement technique that asks, "Why did it happen?" in cases of unnecessary disease, unnecessary disability, or untimely death ("negative indexes of health"). It also provides a list of sentinel health events which would prompt investigation.

Rosenberg, S. N.; Gunston, C.; Berenson, L.; and Klein, A. "An Eclectic Approach to Quality Control in Fee-for-Service Health

Care: The New York City Medicaid Experience." *American Journal of Public Health* 66(1976): 21–30.

New York City Medicaid has established a comprehensive system for monitoring excess charges and bad practices of physicians. Items, such as the following, are flagged: 1) x-rays that equal or exceed 25% of the number of office visits, and 2) drug abuse items and narcotics that number more than 3% of all prescriptions. This technique is used to contain costs and to detect fraud and malpractice.

Talley, R. B., and Laventurier, M. F. "Drug Utilization and Peer Review in San Joaquin." *Quality Assurance of Medical Care.* Regional Medical Programs Service: HEW Monograph, February 1973, pp. 287–311.

The San Joaquin Foundation for Medical Care, responsible for administering the State Medicaid program in four California counties, has instituted a computerized review system of drug-prescribing patterns. The system furnishes the following reports:
1.   a duplicate payment report;
2.   a refill control report;
3.   an appropriate-quantity report;
4.   a physician, pharmacist, and drug profile listed by therapeutic class;
5.   an area drug profile listed by therapeutic class; and
6.   an exceptional patient report.

Irregularities are assessed by a drug utilization review committee composed of four pharmacists and one physician. When indicated, the committee notifies potential pharmacist and physician offenders. This program has yielded a 12.1% savings in drug expenditures. The program has added a component for monitoring adverse drug reactions resulting from drug interactions and has found that 7.57% of the patient population have been exposed to potential drug interactions.

Herxheimer, A. "Sharing the Responsibility for Treatment." *Lancet* 2(1976): 1294.

**Questions Which Patients May Want to Ask the Doctor
about Their Treatment**

You will get most benefit from your treatment if you know why you are having it and how you should use it. So if there are any questions on this sheet that concern you and that you don't know the answer to, please ask the doctor.

1.   *What for and how?*
      What kind of tablets are they and in what way do you expect them to help?
      How should I take them?
      Will I be able to tell whether they are working?

2.   *How important?*
      How important is it for me to take these tablets?
      What is likely to happen if I do not take them?

3.   *Any side-effects?*
      Do the tablets have any other effects that I should look out for? Do they ever cause any trouble?
      Is it all right to drive while I'm taking them?
      Are they all right to take with other medicines I may need?
      Will alcohol interfere with them?

4.   *How long for?*
      How long will I need to continue with these tablets?
      What should I do with any that are left over?
      When will I need to see you again?
      What will you want to know at that time?

Herxheimer, A. "Towards Parity for Therapeutics in Clinical Teaching." *Lancet* 2(1976): 1186–1187.

The author develops a teaching package on drugs for all health workers. While addressed to analysis of any one drug a patient receives, the list of self-assessment questions can be used for an error-audit:

1. Drug name (generic)?
2. Drug class?
3. Route and dose? Child safety cap?
4. Duration of Rx? Expiration date? Refill/policy/drug?
5. How were achievements monitored?
6. What was to be achieved with the drug?
7. What is the drug metabolism, and does the patient have contraindications (liver, kidney, allergic disease)?
8. What are the major side effects of the drug, and were they monitored?
9. What major interactions with other drugs exist, and were these monitored?
10. What was the cost of the drug? Could the patient afford it?
11. Could other drugs have been used?
12. What was the patient told about the drug? What does he believe, remember? Is more information needed?
13. How well has the patient taken the drug? (Taking over 80% of a prescription is defined as compliance.)

Organizational Review

Morehead, M. *Ambulatory Health Care Services*. Springfield, Va.: National Technical Information Service, PB-226 783, 1973.

The Morehead Audit establishes the following data base (each item expanded in great detail) for health centers:

1. target-area community, population and center accessibility (15 items);
2. estimate of active patients (3 items);
3. physical facilities and equipment (17 items);
4. patient flow (clinic mapping);
5. patient eligibility and registration (17 items);
6. appointment system (18 items);
7. patient acceptance and understanding (8 items);
8. program management and administration (16 items);
9. business and fiscal administration (13 items);
10. purchasing and central supply (11 items);
11. personnel administration (17 items);
12. program analysis and reporting (12 items);
13. medical care organization (12 items);
14. family-oriented care organization (9 items);
15. team-oriented care organization (9 items);
16. provider staffing and productivity (5 items);
17. appointments, walk-ins, actual hours (8 items);
18. back-up hospital relationships (21 items);
19. relationships with other community programs (10 items);
20. medical audit (adult, pediatric, OB-Gyn, surgery, dental, psychosocial);
21. nursing, mid-level practitioner assessment (49 items);
22. training and utilization program for new health workers (28 items);
23. medical records assessment (13 items);
24. transportation (18 items);
25. laboratory services (14 items);

26. pharmacy services (26 items);
27. radiology services (11 items);
28. nutrition services (16 items);
29. physical medicine and rehabilitation (14 items);
30. environmental services (10 items); and
31. community participation (43 items).

Thirteen to fifteen persons working five days were needed to do the full assessment.

Comment: The technique uncovers many problems because problems always exist, but no priority or weighting of problems is given. The utility of a single-sweep external audit is unproved.

Morehead, M. A., and Donaldson, R. "Quality of Clinical Management of Disease in Comprehensive Neighborhood Health Centers." *Medical Care* 12(1974): 301–315.

The study is a peer review of the management of patients with serious or potentially serious illness at 40 Neighborhood Health Centers. The major deficiencies were in medical management systems, lack of follow-up of positive lab and x-ray findings (due to broken appointments, lack of continuity, etc.), poor liaison with hospitals, poor patient compliance (for social and educational reasons). Physician performance correlated with board certification and strong hospital backup, but only a small portion of poor-quality events were physician-performance related.

Review of Federally Supported Neighborhood Health Centers: *Final Report 1968–1976*. U.S. Department of Health, Education and Welfare, Public Health Service, 1977.

This is the final report of the now-famous Morehead Team that in seven years did 172 comprehensive audits of 97 ambulatory Neighborhood Health Centers. They can now describe trends in management and programs:

(Items of special interest are 8, 11, 12, 18−24.)

1. Center staff now understand eligibility requirements and sliding fee-for-service scales are in use;
2. broken appointments and walk-ins remain at a 40% level, and handling of this problem remains ineffective;
3. records and forms are more satisfactory. The problem-oriented medical record has produced no impressive results. A problem front sheet is useful, however;
4. waiting times are still troublesome, and scheduling systems dysfunctional;
5. patient privacy is seldom rigorously maintained;
6. patient awareness remains low on: services, hours, grievance procedures, community board activities;
7. the Team concept "has been most difficult if not impossible, for most centers to bring about";
8. Clinical Management Scores (Morehead Scale of 100) remain fixed in the 60−79 range ("satisfactory");
9. 2.4 patients are seen per hour per provider;
10. baseline health assessments for adults are still only partially fulfilled;
11. the presence of *adequate administrative support mechanisms* [italics the annotator's] correlated with impressive and comprehensive ambulatory care;
12. *overprescription of antiobiotics and dangerous drugs remains a major problem*;
13. pediatric care and baseline assessments—especially utilizing nurse practitioners—have improved, but deficiencies still exist in: social care, adolescent care, TB and anemia screening, and immunizations;
14. OB-Gyn appears to be the most variable among the NHCs in quality of care;
15. dental programs performed poorly consistently, due to lack of leadership and supervision;
16. nursing remained traditional and without much voice in top management;

17. nutrition services persistently underachieved;
18. psychosocial services have expanded in depth and breadth;
19. data collection remained unsophisticated and data poorly used. Evaluation tended to adhere to HEW guidelines;
20. fiscal administration is more sophisticated in accounting, third-party billing, self-pay and multi-source funding;
21. *clarity of direction* is most often missing (that is, goal setting and negotiation) as is equilibrium between the different power blocs;
22. *performance standards* against which assessments can be made are often not set;
23. *replanning* and reallocation of resources is seldom done well; and
24. community boards are maturing and increasing their helpfulness.

San Agustin, M.; Goldfrank, L.; Matz, R.; Suberman, C.; Hamerman, D.; Bloom, R.; and Pitter, D. "Reorganization of Ambulatory Health Care in an Urban Municipal Hospital." *Archives of Internal Medicine* 136(1976): 1262–1266.

When a Neighborhood Family Health Center (NFHC) was directly integrated with emergency and in-patient services, the following changes in organization occurred:
1. from unsupervised "moonlighting" physicians to primary health care teams;
2. from no follow-up to continuity of care from the emergency room to the NFHC or hospital by the *same resident*;
3. from no supervision or standards to an organized house staff system bridging NFHC, ER, and hospital with regular chart reviews, patient audits and teaching rounds; and
4. from fragmented sub-specialty clinic care to care by primary teams using sub-specialists in consultation only.

The results of the change to a continual, team-oriented, supervised, audited care program were:

1.　statistically significant changes in hospitalizations for:

cerebrovascular accidents　　　−53%
severe hypertension　　　　　　−49%
diabetic coma-acidosis　　　　　−48%
congestive heart failure　　　　−35%
asthma　　　　　　　　　　　　−35%
toxic ingestions (alcohol, drugs)　+36% (deliberate policy)

2.　total out-patient visits were only slightly increased (therefore, not a question of access), and the length of hospitalization was unchanged.

Kerr, M., and Trantow, D. J. "Defining, Measuring, and Assessing the Quality of Health Services." *Public Health Reports* 84(1969): 415–424.

This paper looks at health care from a "macro" level, stating flatly that "differences in individual provider performance levels are expected to balance out within any geographic area" and that variances are further minimized by medical audits utilization review, accreditation, etc. Therefore, the "macro" view of quality should focus on quantity, availability, accessibility, timeliness, adequacy, cost of services, and epidemiologic assessment of local needs.

Zusman, J., and Slawson, M. R. "Service Quality Profile: Development of a Technique for Measuring Quality of Mental Health Services." *Archives of General Psychiatry* 27(1972): 692–698.

Mental health service quality is defined by nine variables:
1.　physical environment;
2.　administrative structure and procedures;
3.　staff training and qualification;

4.   staff commitment and morale;
5.   patient integrity and safety;
6.   relative cost;
7.   appropriateness of treatment;
8.   patient satisfaction; and
9.   short-term outcome (six-months-functional capacity).

The rest of the article details the difficulties in determining criteria, especially for the last three items. The study of "critical incidents" in care (major do's or don'ts) is useful.

Interim User's Guide to the Bureau of Community Health Services Common Reporting Requirements. Bureau of Community Health Services, Health Services Administration, DHEW, Rockville, Maryland, May 1977.

The federal government requires health centers funded by the Bureau of Community Health Services (BCHS) to submit data in a common format now popularly called the "BCRR" (BCHS Common Reporting Requirements).

These data force each center to monitor itself and provide a regional and national basis for comparing and standardizing performance.

Four areas are covered by the BCRR:
1.   project utilization and growth;
2.   provider staffing and productivity;
3.   cost and efficiency analyses; and
4.   financial management.
Each has a series of ratios that provide management-oriented information. The data are gathered every 3–6 months.

Comment: The system got under way in 1977 and will undoubtedly require adjustments. At least two revisions have come out since 1977 which emphasize only a few items.

Indicator

A.
Project
Utilization
and
Growth

1. $\dfrac{\text{Actual users}}{\text{Projected users}} \times 100$

2. $\dfrac{\text{Actual users}}{\text{Target population}} \times 100$

3. $\dfrac{\text{New medical users}}{\text{Total medical users}}$

4. $\dfrac{\text{New dental users}}{\text{Total dental users}}$

5. $\dfrac{\text{Average \# medical encounters}}{\text{Medical user}}$

6. $\dfrac{\text{Average \# dental encounters}}{\text{Dental user}}$

B.
Provider
Staffing
and
Productivity

1. $\dfrac{\text{Medical users}}{\text{Medical providers}}$

2. $\dfrac{\text{Dental users}}{\text{Dental providers}}$

3. $\dfrac{\text{Encounters per year}}{\text{Full-time physicians}}$

4. $\dfrac{\text{Encounters}}{\text{Full-time mid-level practitioner}}$

5. $\dfrac{\text{Non-provider support staff}}{\text{Physician and } \frac{1}{2} \text{ MLPs}}$

6. $\dfrac{\text{Family planning encounters}}{\text{Family planning user}}$

C.
Cost and
Efficiency

1. $\dfrac{\text{Average cost}}{\text{Medical user}}$
(all medical costs)

Meaning	Suggested Standard
Relation of budget and staffing to planning	90–100% (<90% = overstaffed >100% = understaffed)
Access, especially for high-risk groups	Improvement over time
Growth rate of a center	New center: >0.5 Older center: <0.5
Same	Same
Measures utilization (should be made target-group specific)	1.5–3.0 per 6 months (<1.5 = underutilization >3.0 = overutilization)
Same	None
Measures utilization and staffing	1,000–1,500 (<1,000 = overstaffed or underutilized >1,500 = understaffed or mostly episodic care)
Same	Same
Productivity	4,200 (2,800 for new centers)
Same	2,100 (1,400 for new centers)
One source of excessive administrative cost	No more than 3
Measures utilization	None
Measure of utilization and efficient use of resources	Decrease over time

Indicator

2. $\dfrac{\text{Average cost}}{\text{Dental user}}$

3. $\dfrac{\text{Average cost}}{\text{Medical encounter}}$

4. $\dfrac{\text{Average cost}}{\text{Dental encounter}}$

5. $\dfrac{\text{Administrative/Housekeeping/Maintenance cost}}{\text{Total ambulatory care cost}} \times 100$

6. $\dfrac{\text{Direct health care cost}}{\text{Total ambulatory care cost}} \times 100$

7. $\dfrac{\text{Support activities cost}}{\text{Total ambulatory care cost}} \times 100$

D.
Financial
and
Management

1. $\dfrac{\text{Collections \& adjustments}}{\text{Total charges}} \times 100$

2. $\dfrac{\text{Adjustments}}{\text{Total charges}} \times 100$

3. $\dfrac{\text{Charges}}{\text{Reimbursable costs}} \times 100$

4. $\dfrac{\text{Collections}}{\text{Total ambulatory care costs}} \times 100$

5. $\dfrac{\text{Actual revenue}}{\text{Projected revenue}} \times 100$

6. $\dfrac{\text{Actual expenditure}}{\text{Projected expenditure}} \times 100$

7. $\dfrac{\text{Total revenue}}{\text{Total expenditure}} \times 100$

Meaning	Suggested Standard
Same	Same
Same	Same
Same	Same
Measure of efficiency, availability and use of resources	20% (up to 30% in first year)
Same	60–70%
Proportion of costs devoted to medical records, transport, marketing, etc.	10–20%
Measures efficiency of billing and collection	Approach 100%
Indicator of cash flow	Approach 10%
Measure how closely fee schedule matches cost of services	Approach 100%
Reflection of grant-support, and non-reimbursable costs	Decrease grant dependency
Measure of planning, monitor of shortfall.	Approach 100%
Measure of planning, monitor of spending and level of operation.	Approach 100%
Financial solvency (bottom line)	If <100% determine why If >100% determine what to do with excess.

Stearns, N. S.; Bergan, T. A.; Roberts, E. B.; and Quigley, J. L. "Systems Intervention: New Help for Hospitals." *Health Care Management Review* 1(1976): 9–18.

A "systems" approach to overall quality is described in the rehabilitation of a medical residency program. What's illustrated is the interdependence of functions and persons (see the system flow diagram, below, used as a tool for problem analysis). Analysis and solution of problems require: 1) a wide forum of people involved in the different parts of the system; 2) a focus on specific problems; 3) use of the flow diagrams to illustrate interdependencies; and 4) orientation to change. Those most likely to resist change are asked to take responsibility for seeing that it happens.

FIGURE 2   A MORE COMPLETE VIEW OF SOME OF THE FACTORS IN-
FLUENCING THE ADEQUACY OF ANCILLARY SERVICES AND
THE QUALITY OF TEACHING

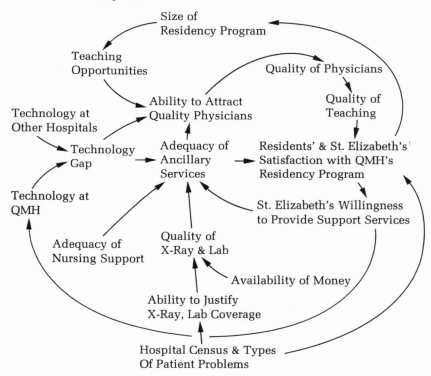

FIGURE 3
ATTRACTIVENESS OF QMH TO PHYSICIANS AND THE NEED TO HIRE
PHYSICIANS

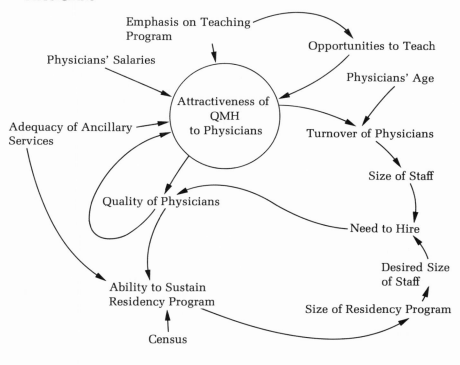

Paxton, G. "Comprehensive Outpatient Audit Systems." Part I in *Insights and Issues: A Volume of Selected Proceedings from a National Series of Conferences for Neighborhood Health Center Medical Directors*, edited by W. J. Manseau, pp. 48–52. Washington, D.C.: The National Association of Neighborhood Health Centers, 1975.

The Denver Neighborhood Health Program sends 120,000 people through its facilities, including a general hospital. A single outpatient chart is used in a computerized system. Three types of audit are used:

1.   an administrative audit which relates to chart availability, record linkages, rates of missed appointments and their follow-up, determination of continuity of care, waiting time, and clinic flows;
2.   a medical audit which employs the standard tracer method;
3.   a medical management audit which is an inventory of services and problems such as:
    a) practice profile by problem;
    b) total patient report as he/she moves through the system;
    c) practice profile by diagnosis;
    d) drug prescription profiles related to problems;
    e) laboratory reports related to diagnoses and problems; and
    f) communicable disease report.
No data on the utility or use of reports are given.

St. Clair, C. H.; Silver, M. J.; and Spivack, G. "An Instrument to Assess Staff Time Utilization in a Community Health Center." *Community Mental Health Journal* 11(1975): 371–380.

This method is meant to help centers where the staff cannot accomplish what is expected of them, and it is necessary to see if the expectations are unreasonable.

A daily staff log was used to list staff hours spent in direct patient and collateral contact, clinical backup, consultation, education, and administration in a community mental health center. Data in the log was compared across disciplines, before and after administrative changes, and in the course of cost-effectiveness studies. During the first year of use of this log at the test site, more staff time was spent in clinical activities, and more fees were collected. Such a log can be the basis for program cost-allocations and cost-analyses.

Luce, B. R., and Stamps, P. L. "An Approach to Accessibility Analysis." *American Journal of Public Health* 66(1976): 581–582.

The study used the Census Bureau DIME file, a directory which assigns a geographic code to all addresses; census tract data available also includes average family size, income, age, ethnicity, sex, and welfare status. These can be compared to the Center's patient population to determine positive and negative access profiles.

Pozen, M. W., and Bonnet, P. D. "Effectiveness of Educational and Administrative Interventions in Medical Outpatient Clinics." *American Journal of Public Health* 66(1976): 151–155.

A study in a city hospital emergency room was done in three clinics. Clinic 1 had intensive education of house officers by faculty. Clinic 2 had a marked increase in administrative support (records, follow-up, appointments, lab slips). Clinic 3 was "traditional." The results showed no change in adequacy of process (¾ good or excellent), or outcome (50% improvable), or patient satisfaction (high in all clinics). The education clinic was more satisfying to the house officers; the administrative clinic produced better chart retrieval, appointment keeping, and follow-up than did the other two.

"Guidance for Internal Quality Assessment." Bureau of Community Health Services, DHEW, Rockville, Maryland, 1977.

This document is a draft put out by the Bureau of Community Health Services, DHEW. It is not official or final but is annotated here to indicate the direction of federal thought on Quality-of-Care and its Assessment.
"Quality" is defined in two categories:
Program Quality and Technical Quality
The dimensions of Program Quality are:
1.   accessibility of care;
2.   comprehensiveness of care (meaning availability and integration of services);

3.   continuity of care (including record linkages);
4.   efficiency of care (meaning cost-effectiveness and fiscal soundness); and
5.   patient participation in care.

Ambulatory Health Care Standards (not yet in final form) are the norms to be followed and measured against. Program Quality is to be administered by a center-wide committee.

Technical Quality is reviewed by providers and involves peer review, and review of support services. Any number of internal or external audit mechanisms may be used. Quality Assurance is not touched on.

"Working Paper on the *Definition of Quality of Health Care Services.*" Seattle, Wash.: The Quality Improvement Workgroup, Public Health Service, Region X, 1977.

A Working Paper from Region X's Quality Improvement Workgroup defines quality-of-care with the following *dimensions* and *objectives*:

1.   CLINICAL APPROPRIATENESS
      (Staff qualifications, on-going education, preventive care, improved health, minimal hazard, satisfied patients, patient awareness, compliance, and self-care, accurate decisions on diagnosis and therapy, art of "caring")

2.   ACCOUNTABILITY
      (Assurance mechanisms to promote patient, staff and governing board accountability for follow-up care, and provision of service, respectively)

3.   COMPREHENSIVENESS
      (Community orientation, including environmental issues, family orientation, availability and linkage of services and disciplines)

4.   CONTINUITY
      (Principal provider or team responsibility, supportive communications and records, joint provider-patient health care plans)

5.   EFFICIENCY
      (National norms for: cost/unit service or episode produc-
      tivity, compensation and satisfaction of provider, clinic
      flow, good fiscal practice, service integration)
6.   ACCESSIBILITY
      (No barriers to care, no interruption in moving to another
      level of care, cultural relevance, convenience)

**Hirschhorn, N.; Klein, S. F.; McCormack, J.; Lamstein, J. H.; and
Warner, T. N.** "Quality by Objectives: A Model of Quality Health
Care Assessment and Assurance for Ambulatory Health Centers."
The Journal of Ambulatory Care Management 1(1978): 55–73.

The paper highlights the problems of current approaches to
quality-of-care assessment and assurance:
1.   no agreement exists on the precise attributes of "good care";
2.   methods of assessing care are imprecise, not replicable, or
      measure attributes that are irrelevant to what happens to a
      patient;
3.   most assessments focus too narrowly on the medical/techni-
      cal aspects of care;
4.   measurements that are imprecise, irrelevant, or too narrowly
      focused further distort the definition of "good care";
5.   assessment methods that try to measure organizational weak-
      nesses do so by "rolling back" from errors found in a chart
      audit, and hunting down deficits in the various systems
      (client, provider, organization, etc.); this is an inefficient pro-
      cess;
6.   health care providers seldom take remedial action ("assur-
      ance") based on the results of assessment; and
7.   even if full compliance with current notions of "quality"
      were made, this could result in unacceptable doubling or
      tripling of costs of ambulatory care.
The authors then suggest that some attributes of good care or
"Dimensions of Care" are known; that these can be specified in a
management by objectives framework with criteria, and quantified

as targets; that, if these dimensions, criteria and targets are agreed to by various parties involved in health centers, and the targets are met, considerable improvement in health care and health is likely. The dimensions, criteria and targets tend to be those already being specified by funding agencies and professionals alike, and many form the basis of both program and resource management. The dimensions suggested are (each with a number of specific sub-elements):

1.   access;
2.   availability;
3.   acceptability;
4.   minimum medical standards; and
5.   cost effectiveness and efficiency.

Other possible dimensions include community development, holistic medicine, health education, and self-care.

Strumpf, G. B., and Garramone, M. A. "Why Some HMOs Develop Slowly." *Public Health Reports* 91(1976): 496–503.

By 1976, 175 pre-paid health maintenance organizations were in existence, with six million members, over a third belonging to California's Kaiser Plans. A total of 66 projects failed either in the planning or development stage. The principal reasons were:

1.   poor management;
2.   poor motivation and understanding of HMO goals by both sponsoring agency and community; and
3.   poor recruitment of providers.

Sims, N. H. "Clinic Self-Evaluation Manual for the Determination and Improvement of Clinic Efficiency." Baltimore, Md.: Johns Hopkins University and Westinghouse Electric Corporation, 1971.

The manual weds industrial efficiency technology to health center operations. While the vocabulary may be off-putting to most health centers ("queuing theory," "performance matrix," "variability coefficient," etc.), several useful techniques of setting goals and targets, setting priorities, measuring patient flow, measuring productivity, and analyzing work content are presented.

In addition, some prescriptive help in interpreting the data is given.

Hirschhorn, N.; Lamstein, J.; Klein, S.; McCormack, J.; and Goldberg, R. "Quality by Objectives. A Practical Method for Quality of Care Assessment and Assurance. A Self-Instructional Manual." Boston: G. K. Hall & Co., 1978.

This manual is designed around a classic case-study, "The Perils of Harmony Heights Neighborhood Health Center." Its main lesson is that quality is an organization-wide concern, not just the review of medical charts. The content has two parts: a model based on a simple adaptation of management-by-objectives, and much prescriptive material in terms of likely goals, criteria, targets, methods of assessment, and ideas for assurance. Criteria and targets are written about five "dimensions of care": access, availability, acceptability, adequacy (minimal medical standards in treatment and prevention), and cost-effectiveness and efficiency. The thesis— borne out by field experience—is that meeting the criteria of these dimensions goes a long way toward assuring a quality program.

Medical Records

Medical Records

THE PROBLEMS WITH MEDICAL RECORDS

Long, T., and Rogers, K. D. "A Limitation in the Use of Office Records for Health Care Evaluation." *Pediatrics* 56(1975): 295–296.

A potential limitation of physician office records for ambulatory health care evaluation is their completeness. This study observed 6 physicians in a suburban group practice caring for 17 patients with possible streptococcal sore throat. What the physicians actually did was then compared with what was written in the patients' charts. Both functions and records were assessed according to a list of criteria acceptable to these six providers.

Many functions performed by providers were not recorded. Nor could compliance with treatment be determined from the charts.

	Mean % Performed	Mean % Recorded
History (5 items)	64	32
Physical (5 items)	89	61
Throat Culture	100	94
Instructions & Follow-up (3 items)	33	0
Treatment Compliance	unknown	unknown

Instructions and follow-up are the key links to continuity of patient care and the "art of caring." These were the tasks performed most poorly.

Zuckerman, A. E.; Starfield, B.; Hochreiter, C.; and Kovasznay, B. "Validating the Content of Pediatric Outpatient Medical Records

185

by Means of Tape-Recording Doctor-Patient Encounters." *Pediatrics* 56(1975): 407–411.

Fifty-one encounters between three university clinic pediatricians serving an immediate group were recorded on tape and the content of the encounters was compared to the content of the medical record. Results were similar for all three physicians.

	% Present on Tape & Chart	% Present on Tapes Only	% Present on Chart Only	% Absent on Both
Chief Complaint	96	0	4	0
Diagnosis	69	0	28	3
Drug Name	28	0	66	6
Dosage	32	37	5	26
Actions	3	52	0	45
Side Effects	0	8	0	92 *
Degree of Disability	15	10	4	71 *
Studies	24	0	2	74
Appointments	39	0	0	61 *
Follow-up Indications	12	31	0	57 *
Allergies	2	12	0	86 *

The average time spent per patient was 10 minutes. One distressing result is the degree of non-performance (last column) in some critical areas (starred): history, patient communication, and follow-up. Patients' knowledge significantly improved if these items were present both in the tape and in the chart.

Fessel, W. J., and Van Brunt, E. E. "Assessing Quality of Care from the Medical Record." *The New England Journal of Medicine* 286(1972): 134–138.

In light of the criticisms which can be made of the medical record audit, studies were conducted in three hospitals to determine the relationship, if any, between the recorded processes of medical care and the outcome of that care. Information was abstracted from patients' records by a medical record librarian; her accuracy was checked and a 2.4% error rate found.

Fifty charts of appendectomy patients in each hospital were audited for eight commonly sought signs or symptoms. Although a significant disparity was found in the data from hospital to hospital, patient outcomes were the same in all three hospitals.

Fifty records of patients with acute myocardial infarction were studied from one hospital and were audited by two sets of criteria:
1.   a process list of 44 items; and
2.   a process list of 10 items found in previous studies to be related to survival or death.

Two additional sets of 50 charts (one set = survived and uncomplicated; the other = died) were audited by a list of 26 explicit process criteria drawn up by three hospital cardiologists.

As with appendectomy, no significant relation existed between the audit scores and any of the post-hospital outcomes for myocardial infarction.

These findings show that neither quality nor quantity of recorded data was related to outcomes for either of the two conditions. The authors conclude that chart audits do not reflect standards of care, nor do explicit lists of process criteria relate to outcomes.

Thompson, H. C., and Osborne, C. E. "Office Records in the Evaluation of Quality of Care." *Medical Care* 14(1976): 294–314.

Ten thousand five hundred charts of 166 pediatricians and family physicians were audited for child health supervision and for three diseases—pharyngitis, asthma, and urinary tract infection in girls. They were assessed mainly for documentation of criteria.

Indicator	Average % Clients with Documentation
1. Health Supervision	
History	33
Growth and Development	73
Screening	56
Counseling	18
2. Diseases	
History	50
Physical	49
Lab	69
Treatment	63
Counseling	25
Follow-up	42

Fifty-two percent of the 166 physicians said that they did more than they recorded. Pediatricians and group practices recorded better than solo and family physicians. This study suggests that valid peer review may be impossible with current levels of record keeping.

NEW APPROACHES TO MEDICAL RECORDS

McDonald, C. J.; Murray, R.; Jeris, D.; Bhargava, B.; Seeger, J.; and Blevins, L. "A Computer-Based Record and Clinical Monitoring System for Ambulatory Care." *American Journal of Public Health* 67(1977): 240–245.

The Regenstrief Medical Record system is a computer-based system that contains objective subjective data on each patient encountered. It is used to present the data to the clinician in compact reports and to further remind the physician to take various actions. These reminders are generated by physician-authored protocols. Sample reminders are given below:

TABLE 1—SAMPLE OF PROTOCOLS NOW OPERATIVE IN OUR CLINIC

1) *Detection of Potential Drug Interactions*
   If on "mercaptopurine" and on "allopurinol" then reduce dosage of "mercaptopurine" because allopurinol blocks its catabolism.

2) *Inference of Diagnoses*
   If last "tonometry" greater than 23 then consider "diagnosis" glaucoma. Refer to ophthalmology.

3) *Adjustment of Medication Dosage to Take into Account Decreased Excretory Function*
   If on "digoxin" greater than .24 mg. and last BUN greater than 25, then reduce "digoxin" because of increased risk of toxicity.

4) *Detection of Adverse Drug-Disease Interactions*
   If on "propranalol" and on "asthma meds" then reconsider the use of "propranalol" because of aggravation of asthma.

5) *Initiation of Interval Screening*
   If last "cervical pap" before 1 year ago then order "cervical pap."

6) *Adjustment of Therapy to Achieve Objective Goals*
   If last "dias BP sitting" greater than 100 and on "BP meds" then increase dosage of "BP meds" if today's BP high.

7) *Initiation of the Work-up for an Isolated Abnormality*
   If last "HCT" less than 38 or last "HGB" is less than 11.5 and no "blood indices" then order "blood indices" to work up anemia.

8) *Assurance of the Proper Outcome Measures to Follow-up and Assess Therapy*
   If on "angina meds" then observe "angina spells."

The cost of the system is about two dollars per visit. Compared to conventional charting, no differences were observed in time spent with the record or the patient. Compliance with criteria doubled (22 to 51% and 13 to 28% in two separate reports). The cost of health care due to the extra compliance is unrecorded.

Wirtschafter, D. D., and Mesel, E. "A Strategy for Redesigning the Medical Record for Quality Assurance." *Medical Care* 14(1976): 68–76.

Current medical record designs do not help achieve medical care goals. Any information system should be designed to include a feedback loop which would consist of:
1.   monitoring a few indicators;

WIRTSCHAFTER AND MESEL

JOHN DOE   12345-0

PROBLEM

#1 ESSENTIAL HYPERTENSION—FOLLOW-UP VISIT (6TH MONTH)

SUBJ: NEW SYMPTOMS
        DYSPNEA ON EXERTION   __N __Y
        OTHER   __N __Y
        MEDICATION SIDE-EFFECTS
        THIAZIDE–MUSCLE WEAKNESS   __N __Y

        GUANETHIDINE–SYNCOPE   __N __Y
                    –DIARRHEA   __N __Y
                    –FLUID RETENTION   __N __Y
        PATIENT COMPLIANCE
        NO ADDED SALT DIET   __FAIR __POOR
        TAKING MEDS   __GOOD __FAIR __POOR

OBJ: PHYSICAL EXAMINATION
        TODAY'S BP (LYING) __/__
        GOAL BP   "   160/90
                    ABOVE GOAL?   __N __Y
        BP (STANDING) __/__ SYNCOPE?   __N __Y
        HEART–   __NL __ABN

ASMT:DX-ESSENTIAL HYPERTENSION
        __TENTATIVE __FINAL

        RESPONSE TO THERAPY
        __GOOD __FAIR __POOR

2. comparing measurements against standards; and
3. making changes to bring indicators to the level of standards.

The authors believe that certain patient-related outcomes—such as longevity, activity, comfort, satisfaction, stage of illness, coping, and achievement—form a useful set of indicators. A record form may be designed that is both oriented to these indicators and is suitable for chronic illness and health surveillance. An example follows.

FIG. 1. Western Health Clinic encounter form.

DATE OF VISIT: ___/___/___

ACTION

___ORDER SERUM K
___ORDER K SUPPL
___RX CHANGE:

___APPT WITH DIETICIAN
___REINSTRUCTED
___PHN HOME VISIT

___RX CHANGES:

PLAN:
DX___SERUM K
   ___SERUM URIC ACID
   ___BLOOD GLUCOSE
RETURN VISIT:
   ___DAYS; ___WEEKS;
   ___FURTHER DX WORK-UP
   ___RX FOLLOW-UP VISIT

Pollak, V. E.; Buncher, C. R.; and Donovan, E. R. "On-Line Computerized Data Handling System for Treating Patients with Renal Disease." *Archives of Internal Medicine* 137(1977): 446–456.

The development of "source-oriented" and "problem-oriented" charts has been followed by charts that present hard data in "time-oriented" sequences. These sequences are:
1.   serial symptom review;
2.   serial physical findings;
3.   serial laboratory tests; and
4.   serial drug prescriptions.
The system has room for narrative notes which record opinion and reasoning. The advantages of this format are:
1.   interrelationships of events—symptoms and drugs, for example—become quite easy to perceive and audit (faster than the other systems);
2.   other providers can tune in to the progress of a patient rapidly;
3.   research is more easily done; and
4.   computerization of the forms is easy.
The cost—including computers—is 1 to 2% of total patient care costs. This method is only useful for continuing, not episodic care.

Fries, James F., M.D. "Alternatives in Medical Record Formats." *Medical Care* 12(1974): 871–881.

This article compares five record forms for speed of data retrievability:
1.   traditional Outpatient;
2.   traditional Inpatient;
3.   problem oriented Outpatient;
4.   problem oriented Inpatient; and
5.   time-oriented.
A time-oriented chart uses a fixed-format flow-sheet organization showing serial entries of data in all areas—history, physical,

lab data, and drug use. Retrievability was four to five times as fast compared to other formats.

Komaroff, A. L. Protocols for New Health Practitioners: Implications and Experience. In *Design and Use of Protocols*, edited by M. Kallstrom and S. Yarnall, pp. 47–61, Seattle: Medical Computer Services Association, 1975.

Decision logic-tree protocols (algorithms) are guidelines that, based on predominantly "yes-no" answers to specific questions, specify an action. This method is displayed with boxes, arrows, and loops. Such protocols follow the logic of good care without being an irrelevant laundry list. They are used to teach and to audit. Examples are given in the article.

Komaroff, A. L. Audit of Quality and Cost Through Using Protocols. In *Design and Use of Protocols*, edited by M. Kallstrom and S. Yarnall. Seattle: Medical Computer Services Association, 1975.

Logical flow protocols can be readily audited for faulty logic, omissions, or misdiagnoses. Two examples of such errors are: 1) a complaint of dysuria is recorded, but urinalysis is not done; and 2) the diagnosis of strep throat is made but fever, adenopathy, or exudate were not found. Audits also identify times where a deliberate decision to override the protocol was made. These decisions are prompted by such factors as professional judgment and an uncommon event not covered in a protocol. Audits spotlight these cases for further attention. Audits do not pick up adequacy of data collection. However, they do reveal systematic errors that have occurred because of one person. Protocols can be made part of a general information system which can supply data for research.

Cassel, C. "A Diagnostic Index of Clinical Practice." *Journal of the American Medical Association* 237(1977): 663–667.

Individual clinicians can keep track of the categories of illness they see as well as of special topics, such as deaths and problems. The index proposed is alphabetic by organ system, diagnostic procedures, and particular topics, such as "drug reaction." Cross-indexing is done manually. Outcomes, complications, and follow-up are listed.

Yarnall, S. R. "The Problem-Oriented Approach—A *Sine Qua Non* for Audit." In *The Changing Health Care Team: Improving Effectiveness in Patient Care*, edited by S. Zoog and S. Yarnall. Seattle: Medical Communications and Services Association, 1976.

The POMR (Problem Oriented Medical Record) is touted as the only proper vehicle for audit. The article states that audit of "non-problem-oriented records is really an exercise in futility" because of the following features of the POMR:

1. *Database*   (how problems are looked for, how patient is treated as a whole)
2. *Problem List*   (continuity and format)
3. *SOAP Format*   (review of errors of omission and commission)
4. *Integrated Multi-*   (review of team-care and possible system
    Provider Notes   failure)

The author also distinguishes between short loop and long loop audits. The first type require immediate repair; the second are long-range systems' errors or errors caused by insufficient knowledge.

Goldfinger, S. E. "The Problem-Oriented Record: A Critique from a Believer." *The New England Journal of Medicine* 288(1973): 606–608.

This article is a critique of the problem-oriented medical record from a user who is concerned with its oversell. The limitations of this record are:

1. POMR adherents overemphasize style, against content;
2. information retrieval is probably slower, especially when all provider notes, of mixed quality, are chronologically intermingled;
3. there is no certainty that "data base" is accurate, necessary or defensible;
4. synthesis of individual "problems" into a single entity may be retarded by compartmentalization;
5. problem lists can be shuffled and changed using identical data; for example, do "atypical ECG tracing" plus "vague chest pain" equal "heart disease"?; and
6. audits are not necessarily helped by POMR, because POMR does not guarantee complete recording.

Comment: Listing of separate "problems" has led to separate treatments and medicines for each "problem."

Switz, D. M. "The Problem-Oriented Medical Record." *Archives of Internal Medicine* 136(1976): 1119–1123.

Compared to standard source-oriented records, use of the problem-oriented medical record at a V.A. teaching hospital had no beneficial effect on the thoroughness of data accumulation, the process of care, or the ease or accuracy of chart audit. The condition studied was anemia.

Fletcher, R. H. "Auditing Problem-Oriented Records and Traditional Records." *The New England Journal of Medicine*, 299(1974): 829–833.

The author compares a controlled study on retrievability of data from problem-oriented medical records (POMR) to the standard "source-oriented" format. In terms of time to read, retrievability of data, and recognition of errors in care (charts read by medical residents), no differences were found.

Hertz, C. G.; Bernheim, J. W.; and Perloff, T. N. "Patient Participation In the Problem-Oriented System: A Health Care Plan." *Medical Care* 14(1976): 77–79.

The authors use a Health Care Plan written in problem-oriented style as a contract with the patient on what he or she expects from care and health maintenance. A copy is given to the patient.

Shenkin, B. N., and Warner, D. C. "Giving the Patient His Medical Record: A Proposal to Improve the System." *The New England Journal of Medicine* 289(1973): 688–692.

The authors offer a proposal that patients be given their in- and out-patient records. The benefits expected are:
1.   improved information to the patient (therefore, compliance);
2.   continuity of care, less fragmentation, or repetition of procedures;
3.   more patient autonomy and therefore better relationships to providers; and
4.   better notes and entries.